Shot Ready

Shot Ready

Stephen Curry

One World
An imprint of Random House
A division of Penguin Random House LLC
1745 Broadway
New York, NY 10019
oneworldlit.com
randomhousebooks.com

Copyright © 2025
by Unanimous Media Holdings, LLC

Penguin Random House values and supports copyright. Copyright fuels creativity, encourages diverse voices, promotes free speech, and creates a vibrant culture. Thank you for buying an authorized edition of this book and for complying with copyright laws by not reproducing, scanning, or distributing any part of it in any form without permission. You are supporting writers and allowing Penguin Random House to continue to publish books for every reader. Please note that no part of this book may be used or reproduced in any manner for the purpose of training artificial intelligence technologies or systems.

ONE WORLD and colophon are registered trademarks of Penguin Random House LLC.

Image credits begin on page 407.

ISBN 978-0-593-59729-3
Ebook ISBN 978-0-593-59730-9

Printed in China

987654321

First Edition

Book design: No Ideas
Creative Director: Erick Peyton
Content Editor: Kalyna Kutny

The authorized representative in the EU for product safety and compliance is Penguin Random House Ireland, Morrison Chambers, 32 Nassau Street, Dublin D02 YH68, Ireland, https://eu-contact.penguin.ie.

I Have a Superpower
I Am Extraordinary

Contents

Preface	XII
Part 1: Rookie	1
Rise Into Your Shot	
Part 2: Leader	187
The Height of the Arc	
Part 3: Veteran	315
Stretching Your Prime	
Acknowledgments	405
Image Credits	407

"I Can Do

ll THINGS..."

Preface

I leave the house early in the morning while my kids are still asleep. It's July, so the school parking lot is empty when I drive in, but I know the code to let myself into the gym. This high-school gym is on the short list of courts I can use in the summers without anybody knowing. The key to these summer workouts, as in most things in life, is getting started before everyone else's day begins.

Usually, I meet my trainer Brandon Payne here and we focus on the technical details of a particular shot that's on my mind. We practice not until I get the shot right, but until I can't get it wrong.

But today, it's going to be just you and me.
With one switch, four lines of fluorescent ceiling lights flicker to life and hum over the hardwood. I give the ball a hard dribble, because even here in the practice gym, intensity and intention are important. Warming up, I look out at the five empty rows of blue pull-out bleachers that line the court—as a kid in an empty gym like this one, I would picture a crowd filling those seats.

It was just this sort of atmosphere—a small gym, away from crowds and distractions—where I put in most of the hours I spent learning the game as a young player. A few years into my career as a Golden State Warrior, I realized these gyms were still where I was most comfortable. Being here now grounds me in the memory of my earliest lessons. No matter how good I feel like I've gotten, I always come back to the basics.

I was never the most gifted athlete—not the highest jumper or the fastest runner or the tallest player on the court. In college, I looked like a middle-schooler trying to age himself up with a mustache so thin it seemed drawn on. Depending on my haircut, I'm still only 6'3" in a league where the average is 6'6".

But the work carried me through. I fell in love with the grind. You have to. With the sacrifices that it takes to be great, you have to find joy in the work you do when no one else is around. I hate when coaches or trainers on the internet talk about "the unseen hours" that go into being successful, because it makes that sort of preparation sound mysterious and secretive. But when I talk about "the grind," I'm simply describing the most important hours in any pursuit, the ones we invest in ourselves. I do this work in the gym in isolation—there's no defense, no live action—but, even alone, I practice with a shot-ready mentality, training as if the stakes are high and the clock is low, so that I can rehearse finding balance in the midst of great intensity. Even in a high-school gym like this one, I can re-create the feeling of a tied NBA game with seconds to go by conjuring the scenario in my imagination and playing through it. I spend so much time practicing in this feeling so that even under the bright lights and crushing pressure of a real game, I can easily fall into an unconscious flow and execute my training. Of course, I'll still feel all the nerves, but I don't let them linger. Instead, they pass right through me. What is left behind is a calm that allows my training to kick in. And then I deliver.

Being shot ready requires practice, training, and repetition, but it rewards that work with an unmatchable feeling of transcendence. My peak experience of joy is when I can lose myself in the poetry and rhythm of a fast-paced game—when there's no time to think, and there are nine other guys flying around me, but I have the ball in my hands and somehow *know* exactly where it is going to go. This joy is only possible because of what I do in this gym, the hours I invest in practice and watching film. And then when the moment of truth arrives, I can let go. It is the ultimate freedom.

Playing at the heightened level of the NBA for 82 games puts me in a state of sustained, concentrated intensity for seven or eight months every year. When the season's over and I come back to a small gym like this, I refresh and return to my basic love of the game. **And a key part of that love of the game—my love of play—is the pleasure I get in finding ways to play better.**

When I'm putting in hours to boost my performance, I don't know exactly how and when it's going to pay off, but I have faith that it will. Even after all these years in the league, I still have these *aha* moments in the middle of a game: I'll see an action or match-up or game situation developing and think, *Oh yeah, back in July we gamed out this exact scenario.* Now I have an advantage. In the crucial seconds that follow, everything slows down for me as my nervous system reacts. I feel a rush of adrenaline, but it's targeted for precision work instead of just flooding my system. My airways open up, adding more oxygen to my blood, because my lungs are already supercharged for efficiency from the breathwork I've practiced. My heart doesn't pound, it simply quickens its beat to pump more of that oxygenated blood through my body. The adrenaline even goes to my eyes, which dilate to see every possibility. My brain processes visual information faster than the speed of thought and sets my muscles into motion, following a ready, proven plan. And I just fly. I might do a double behind-the-back crossover, feel the crowd's anticipation, see the guys on my bench rise as I pull up, and then focus for a split second on the rim as I take a high-pressure shot. The confidence I've gained from my practice keeps me in control. I stay in the moment—in a state of alert calm, intensity, and joy.

    That's the lesson I want to share with you in this book. You can get better at whatever you want. I'm inviting you to stretch your imagination as you think about what that means to you. What do you want? It might be your life's equivalent of layups and free-throws, or you can dream big about hitting game-winners from the logo. But I firmly believe that success is not an accident. **Success may not always look the way you expect, but it's attainable for all of us when the rigor of our preparation and the depth of our belief meet the urgency of the moment.** That's what it means to be shot ready.

In the league, I'm known as someone players can come to for advice. Rookies come to me looking for the secret to consistency, rising stars ask me how to adjust from phenom to leader, and veterans talk to me all the time about how to sustain high levels of performance so we can stretch our prime.

    After I gave one young player advice on his workouts, seven months later he was beating me in Game 4 of a playoff series. People outside the league don't understand why I would risk giving my competition an edge, but players get it. We love the game and want to see it evolve. We're always bouncing back and forth a little bit of wisdom or perspective. Now, I'm not trying to give them *everything*, but I'll give them something they can use—better players make for better games. But at the end of the day, we are still competitors. NBA players are good about balancing those two impulses: I can be boys with you and go to dinner the night before the game, but still kill you the next day.

My instinct to share is also the Sonya Curry in me. My mom founded and ran the Montessori elementary school I attended, so while I learned the art of basketball watching my pops play 16 seasons in the NBA, from my mother I learned about learning. I've watched as she's lovingly tailored lessons to help students live out a potential they didn't even see for themselves. From her, I inherited a desire to use my story to connect with people of different backgrounds and help them solve the puzzle of their own potential. Life is intense—and not just in the NBA. **How do we make sure we are prepared, motivated, resilient, and calm in the midst of chaos? How do we tap into the root of joy, meaning, and blissful transcendence that makes it all worthwhile? How can we be shot ready in everything we do?**

Wherever you're at in life, I'm glad you're in this gym with me now. I'm passing the ball to you. Let's go.

Part 1

Rookie

Rise Into Your Shot

We all have an off-season, a time to retreat for a while from the main action of our lives. It might be your whole summer if you're still in school, or a stolen weekend if you're an adult. It may be five minutes of meditation or prayer in the car before work or after you drop the kids off at school. However we get it—or take it—**this gift of time offers us the chance to either stay where we are or create new possibilities for the next season of life.**

In my off-season I put myself in a quiet gym and break my game down to its basics. Working on fundamentals allows me to see—with clarity and honesty—where I need to grow. In this time away from the world, I expand my possibilities.

Welcome to my practice session.

There are two related concepts that guide me at every practice: **grounding and growth.**

Grounding means returning to the fundamentals of the game, which is important whatever your game is. If you don't master and remaster the basics, you'll always be wasting time compensating for fundamental flaws. That doesn't mean you can't succeed. Maybe you'll get by. Maybe instead of preparing, you wing it and let adrenaline push you through. Maybe instead of learning to delegate, you take on every burden yourself and muddle through. Even if those things work for a little while, the inefficiency of working harder for the same result will keep you from growing to the next level.

Growth is the ultimate objective, but it emerges from grounding. Without mastering the fundamental principles of success, you can still struggle through, but at best you'll be meeting your challenges instead of growing from them.

Let's begin.

I have two skills coaches who are drastically different in their approaches to training.

In the summer, there's Brandon Payne, who focuses on precision shooting mechanics. Brandon understands that when you drill, it's not just about the virtue of repetition but also the value of creating a deep understanding of how your body works. Brandon constantly reminds me that great shooting emerges from one fluid movement that starts in the toes and ends in the fingertips. The feet are the source of the shot's power and precision, so it's critical to maintain all of your weight on the insides of your feet—"playing between your arches," Brandon calls it. Just by looking at the arc of my shot, he can tell how much I'm grounding myself in power. There's that word again. It all begins with grounding.

Brandon can cue me down to the millimeter. He will see a shot go slightly left and call me out for putting weight on my fifth metatarsal—my pinky toe. Because that one little toe out of alignment creates a disturbance in the chain of action that ends with the ball's release. Compensating for that small misalignment means I'll have to twist a hip to try to rebalance, and soon everything I do above my waist is compensating to correct the imbalance in my pinky toe. The shot might still go in, but I've reduced my odds for success.

If you are stuck at a certain level and can't quite break through to the next one, look at your fundamentals. **Are you grounded in power?** What habits have you developed that create a chain reaction of compensating actions? Slow down to examine what you're doing, starting from the smallest variable—whatever your equivalent of the fifth metatarsal is—because being disciplined about small details, and taking joy in the work of getting them right until they're second nature, is how you build consistent success.

I've learned over the years that challenges are the most efficient teachers, so I don't run from them. You need to get used to doing difficult things, so you're not living in fear of things going wrong.

In my summer practices, we don't just passively shoot around. Instead, Brandon invents game situations where I'm shooting against a score number or against the clock. To reinforce my shot-ready mindset, we also try to keep my heart rate at the level it reaches during a game. This adds tremendous value to workouts: First, it allows me to *feel* the stakes of the game in my body, even while we're practicing, but it also allows me to practice controlling my heart rate. In other words, this method is not just about getting used to the feeling of a faster heart rate; it's about learning how to get it to go down again. I've practiced enough breath control that even in the middle of a game, I can calm my heart to a resting rate in one 90-second timeout. **Learning recovery is part of any practice.** We all need it. Whatever your equivalent of a 90-second timeout might be—a day off, a break between meetings, a drive from one work site to another—is downtime you can use for recovery. But believe it or not, you have to practice that kind of productive rest.

That's why Brandon runs drills like "Full Court Star," where I sprint from one side of the court to the other, taking shots from different points behind the arc. At the end of this exhausting drill, I lie down on the court and Brandon places a sandbag on my belly, just under my rib cage. With the weight of the bag pushing down on me, my diaphragm has to work harder to get air, forcing me to take stronger, more efficient breaths. Now when I'm in a game, and there's no sandbag, I can still recall this breathing technique, which calms my mind and speeds physical recovery. The drill is a shooting practice, of course, but also it teaches me to make the most of short bursts of downtime. I am training myself in the art of recovery.

Another skill we add to the toolbox focuses on neurocognitive efficiency: We overload my sensory system so my brain processes information quicker. For instance, Brandon sometimes sets up a system of lights where each light corresponds to a ballhandling move. As the lights flash, I have to interpret the light's meaning, make the ballhandling move, and then touch the light to move on to the next one. An actual game presents a flood of variables that have to be processed at lightning speed. We overload our workouts with split-second decisions so the game slows down for me in the real world.

It boils down to this: **Making life harder in practice makes things easier in life.** Staying shot ready does not have the asterisk of "under ideal circumstances." In the off-season, expand what you can endure so that when the stakes are real, you'll rise to bigger challenges. Brandon is my off-season trainer, but during the season I've got Q.

Bruce "Q" Fraser is the man in the field—one of the assistant coaches on the Warriors—and a master storyteller who keeps me thinking about game situations and flow. He also makes sure that I remember to have fun.

During a pregame warmup, Q will mimic the style of specific opponents. This laid-back, funny guy suddenly transforms into an extremely physical defender risking a foul to give me as little space as possible. He knows how to use that warmup time to put pressure on me and spark my killer instinct so I can lock into a game-speed mentality right away.

Q also understands the rhythm of the season's schedule, so he can help me **balance my workouts with my playing time in a way that allows me to sharpen my tools without exhausting myself.**

I try to avoid going down the rabbit hole of every technique I've learned over the years—we don't usually have that much time. So I try to give them the basics, the two big-ticket items that everybody needs to know.

The first thing I do is look at how their feet are planted when in a shooting position. Young players usually have their feet planted too far apart. It might feel comfortable to have a wide stance when you shoot, but don't do it. **Comfort isn't everything.**

I tell them to bring their feet in a bit toward each other to be shot ready, with all 10 toes pointed at the rim, no matter where you are on the court. That's ideal because your hips and chest will follow the direction of your feet toward the basket, and therefore so will your shot. Now as it happens, when I shoot, my feet point 10 degrees off-center to the left. Every time. That's what's natural to me, but even then, I make sure my toes are pointing in the same direction. You'll find your own balance, but start by practicing the textbook technique before you start adapting it.

If you fix the position of your feet, I know for certain you'll shoot better right away. The greatest shooters use their feet and legs as the foundation for their shot—it's the lower body that begins the shooter's motion, and the rest follows. Plant those arches—knees bent behind those 10 toes pointing at the hoop, hips squared with your shoulders—and draw your power up so you explode off the ground and rise into your shot.

Visualiza
key to w

tion is the
inning.

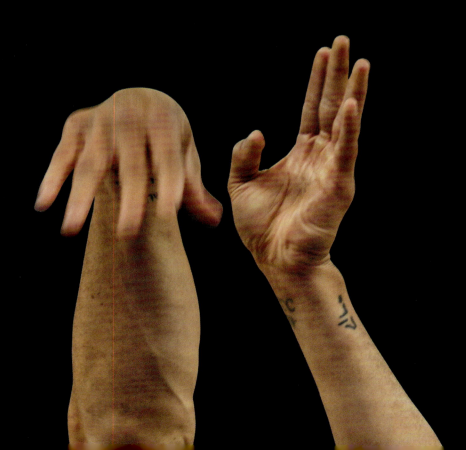

If I have more time to coach you, I'll move to the second big-ticket item: the guide hand. I see people using their less dominant hand way too much when they shoot. I'm a right-handed shooter, so my left hand's only job is to keep the ball in my right hand. I'm really shooting one-handed, and my less dominant hand is just there so the ball doesn't fall. It's not doing *anything*. Some people will have their second hand moving around too much, putting pressure on the ball, inadvertently misguiding it. When you shoot the ball, **every part of you—from your toes to your hips to your right and left hands—has a specific job to do.** One job. If they're doing too much, you'll just be fighting against yourself.

Once you've mastered the mechanics of those two things—the placement of your feet and hands—you can figure out what your own degree of polarity is—that is, where you're comfortable within the range of perfect form. I mentioned I'm 10 degrees off with my feet. I know that keeping your feet directly pointed at the rim is technically better, but my imperfect stance is what comes most naturally to me and it still works, in part because I do the same thing every single time I shoot.

Consistency is sometimes more powerful than technical perfection. Whether it's from two feet or twenty feet, your shot position should always look exactly the same.

When you have mastered the right form—the technically correct way to shoot—then you can relax into your own specific way to do it. And then you need to stick with it.

I'm often asked how it feels or what I'm thinking when I'm in the middle of a game. The truth is that when things are going well, when I have achieved that state of balance within intensity that I train for, I barely have to think or feel at all.

It doesn't matter where my body is in space. I could be moving left, right, backward, forward—it doesn't matter. Guys can be flying at me, hands up, or I could be standing wide open at the top of the arc. No difference. When I'm in balance, I simply let muscle memory and practiced mechanics take over. How do I feel? I feel like I'm never going to miss. What am I thinking? I'm thinking about getting a shot off, but never worrying if it's a good one. It is.

This flow state is the goal of all of the practice. It allows me to play with the kind of freedom that only comes from discipline. In flow, I can let joy and creativity take over. I block out all distractions, even the person guarding me. He can wave his arms and call me every name in the book, but I just smile and wait as the solution to the problem—how to get the ball into the basket—presents itself. When I reach that perfect state of flow, I'm not focused on thoughts or feelings. I'm just hooping.

Once you've reached that state of mind—that zone of complete balance within the intensity of the game—
the joy of the experience will motivate you to do whatever it takes to get back there.

I keep talking about joy in the work for a reason.

    There are 450 NBA players who suit up to play a regular season, every single one of them chasing the same thing: the championship trophy. We each take our own path to that goal, but there is a common oath the best of those players share: We will do our best to outwork everyone else.

    When you're playing at this level, when everyone is keeping that same promise to themselves, or trying to, **what can set you apart is joy.** The ups and downs of any job can steal joy from you—whether it's a day-to-day pilfering or one big disappointment that leaves you wiped out. Protect your passion. It is joy that will sustain your commitment to greatness and the work it requires. But joy is more than a great motivator. It is both the means—the thing that drives your effort—and the end, the glorious payoff of all that work. If you look for it, you will see it as the thread that runs through and supercharges everything.

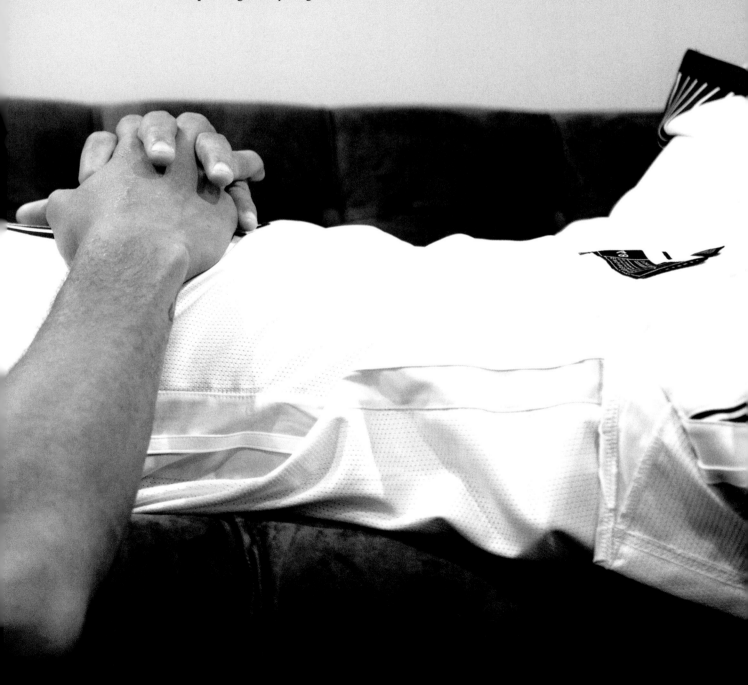

I learned joy early.

In the Toronto Raptors' arena, there's an elevator that takes you from the team locker room to the practice facility on the 300 level. But it's not just an elevator to me: It's a time machine. When I step into that elevator, suddenly I'm 13 again, excitedly ascending to the 300 level with my brother Seth, about to start the next session of our basketball education. Back when the Air Canada Centre was ours.

We'd recently moved from North Carolina to Toronto, where my pops was playing for the Raptors in his last year in the NBA. Dad played 16 years in the league: He was drafted in '86 by Utah, where he played for one season, and then traded to Cleveland for the next; he then spent the next 10 years playing for Charlotte, which is where I grew up—I was born during his third season there. Now he was closing his career on a new team—and we were living in a new country.

My parents were extremely strict about me and my little brother Seth not going to my pops's games on school nights. We'd watch the first half of most games at home until our bedtimes, and then wake up and read the box score in the paper the next morning. But on weekends, when we were lucky enough to go to Raptors games, the arena became our playground. As long as we stuck together—Seth is three years younger than me—we were free to roam. We didn't know at the time that every usher and staff member was looking out for us, too.

If the game was at seven, we'd get there at around 4:30 with my dad. Me and Seth would sit by the bench while the Raptors were doing their pregame warmups. Sometimes we'd go out on the court and rebound for the players, occasionally sneaking off a shot of our own from the corner. About 20 minutes before the game began, the teams would go back into the locker rooms and they'd let us kids come onto the empty floor and shoot around. As fans began to fill the seats, Seth and I would be playing our own little game in front of a few thousand people.

Eventually we'd have to get off the court so the real game could begin. Right after the tip-off, Seth and I would run to the locker room and take the elevator up to the

courts of the practice facility. We were basketball junkies, fiending to play. We'd be up there for the whole first half, getting shots up, playing one-on-one, and just working on our games. Chuck Swirsky's play-by-play would be blasting through the court's PA system, so we'd sometimes re-create the plays he was describing as best we could. Every game we'd pick a different player from the opposing team to mimic: Allen Iverson, Kobe, Shaq, or the Knicks' Mark Jackson, who would eventually be my coach. Each had a patented move that Seth and I would simulate or defend against, living vicariously through these players—the best of the best. Just two spoiled little kids up there hooping.

    Then we'd watch the second half from the upper bowl of the arena. That's where I began to understand how different players approached the game and moved through the action—their court awareness, anticipation, decision-making, and communication—the package of things we now refer to as basketball IQ. I didn't just watch the players on the court. Being in the arena, in the practice gym, and sometimes even in the locker room, I picked up on the differences between the veterans and the rookies, how different players practiced, how they treated their teammates, coaches, the staff, the fans. What kind of energy did they have when they arrived? What kind of energy did they have in the locker room, in warmups? I would then track the results that their energy produced on the court.

    My time in Toronto with my dad and brother was the beginning of my realization that so much of the game is mental. **I noticed that every great player, whether they were a star or a brilliant role player, in their first season or in their tenth, showed the same mental commitment.** No matter how long they'd been playing, the great ones had the confidence that they were the best, but they all wanted to get *better*.

What's the one key ingredient that the greatest shooters have in common?
They all think they're the greatest shooter ever.
To be great, you have to live on that tiny border between confidence and cockiness. But it's your work ethic that earns you that real estate. You can have the most reckless confidence in the world, but if you haven't done the work, it won't mean a thing.

Visualization is the key to winning. You can practice visualization. Do it with me now. Think of yourself taking a shot. At first, you might see yourself from behind, facing a basket. But you have to get closer. Home in. Don't picture yourself on the court. No, get inside your imagined self, see *through* your eyes, and feel through your hands. Notice every detail of your mechanics as you go into a shot. Feel the ball spinning off the leave finger of your hand, feel your hand follow through in a gooseneck. Do it again. Make it perfect. Watch the arc of the ball as it goes exactly where you targeted it, as if the gooseneck of your shooting hand just dropped the ball right in.

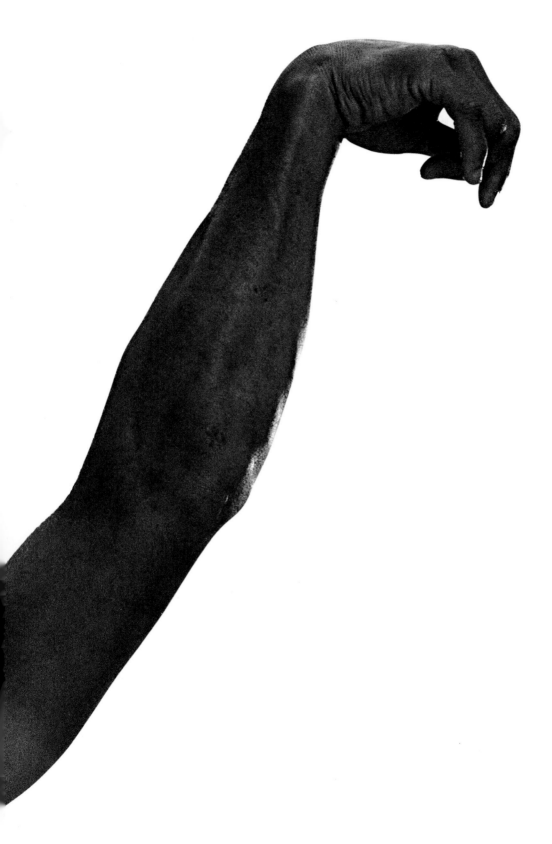

My family moved to Toronto when I was in middle school, but before that I'd played AAU (Amateur Athletic Union) basketball in North Carolina for three years. Up in Toronto, the level of basketball competition was lower than in North Carolina—I wasn't anywhere near the best player in North Carolina, but I was a star in my Queensway middle school. Our team was a Canadian middle-school basketball version of the Bad News Bears—we weren't exactly a team of all-stars, but we bonded as friends. I was a fish out of water—new country, new school, people saying Grade 8 instead of the eighth grade—but basketball quickly connected me to this new world.

I was still pretty short and would shoot threes with a catapult technique, slinging shots from below my waist to get the ball high enough to arc into the basket. My release point was so low that any decent guard could knock my shots down. So, **I relied on finesse and footwork to get space, moving fast to outrun and tire out defenders.** It worked, almost too well. The games started to become middle-school spectacles, with big turnouts for road games in Canada's pockets of basketball culture, Toronto suburbs like Mississauga, Etobicoke, and Scarborough. I started to get a weirdly outsized reputation in that little world: My dad's friend Suresh came to one game where I dropped 60, and people in the crowd thought he was my driver.

That run in Canada ended pretty quickly—that June my dad retired, and we left Canada to go back to North Carolina before the school year even finished. Now that I was back home, I would have to play against tougher competition.

And despite my success in Canada, I had no confidence.

At basketball camps these days I meet a lot of kids around the age of 13. As the parent of a child close to that age, I know the importance of instilling confidence in them at that transitional stage of life. You have to do more than just tell them what their strengths are. You also have to give them confidence to develop new strengths, to try new things and take chances.

I see the kids who come into camp at that age—and even later—and before anything even happens, they're already having an emotional reaction to the new environment and a new learning curve. Sometimes they're visibly apprehensive, already shriveling up, crawling into a shell. The kids I meet in the opening days of camp—boys and girls—have been thinking about this moment for months. I see them with a hand on one hip, then the other, shifting weight from their right leg to their left, heads down. The ones who get the most out of camp are the ones who may come in tense, but who don't get stuck in that space because they're afraid of messing up.

When I get out on the floor with them, I don't pamper them or shy away from bringing competitive energy—it's my way of signaling respect but also dislodging them from being stuck in their nerves. They might even laugh for a second as they realize "Curry is serious here." The surprised delight of that moment is an opening.

Next, I'll remind them of the need to move when they get the ball. "If I get the ball, I'm either catching and shooting, catching and ripping, or catching and giving it up," I say. "If you hold the ball for longer than a second, that's a grenade. It blows up and you're done." The message is: Don't think, do. Make a choice. Act. **You don't reach your potential when you're frozen in place.**

We have the best coaches come in and talk to these kids, and there's always a moment early on when the coach will make an observation after a sprinting drill. Something like, "How many of you are missing shots straight-on from the sprint?" The kids will clam up and find somewhere else to look, usually down. I'll be the first to raise my hand. That's not about being humble—I need to show them that part of championship DNA is acknowledging what you need to work on.

I also want them thinking about their team at home. When I see that a point is really sticking, I'll add, "That's a good one to take back to your team." These are leaders in training—it's not enough for them to improve. They have to help others to succeed, too, if they want to win.

42

When my own children face challenges, I let them stay in that space of discomfort for a little bit. I want them to feel it in their bodies. It's important for them to understand—on that deep level—that sometimes things don't go your way and that I can't control it for them, either. So I ask them to take stock of the things that are under their control: their words, actions, behavior, attitude. Their effort. **In other words, not controlling the discomfort, but controlling how they respond to it.** That is what ultimately defines us.

The decisions you make as a young teen can still offer you lessons decades down the line. When I got back to North Carolina from Toronto to start the ninth grade, I didn't try out for varsity basketball because I was afraid I couldn't compete.

We all have moments in our lives that we look back on and see that we got in our own way. Or times when we've made a choice out of fear of failure or even worse, fear of trying; shrinking from our greatest possibility in favor of something safe. This was one of those times for me and I'll never forget the feeling.

I had already made the decision when my friend Ben Walton walked up to me near the end of the school day.

"Hey, you going to tryouts?"

Varsity basketball tryouts at our high school, Charlotte Christian, were taking place the next Tuesday. Ben was a new guy coming into high school from a public school down the street.

"Nah," I said.

"You're not goin'?" He started questioning me, but I acted like I just didn't care. While I spoke, I looked at him: four or five inches taller than me, and more filled out. He'd be fine. Not me.

Before I left for Toronto, I saw the Charlotte Christian varsity team play every once in a while, and, to put it plainly, they were huge. That was the year they had a bunch of football players on the basketball team and two kids who had since graduated and were now playing Division I basketball in college. They were extremely big and athletic—playing above the rim, dunking, making all these crazily athletic plays. I felt so far removed from that level.

So I made a different plan: play JV my sophomore year, pray to grow a bit, and then maybe try out the next year.

Halfway through my JV year, it was clear to me that I'd made a mistake. I was good enough to play at the next level, but my belief in myself had faltered.

Then during a state playoff against Ravenscroft High School, Coach Shonn Brown subbed me in as a JV call-up. I had a really good four-minute run, and I thought, *I've been missing out on this all year.* But it was my own fault. **I'd shrunk from the challenge. Lesson learned.**

I promised myself I would never betray myself like that again.

To this day, I sometimes wish I was a more physically imposing player. There are a lot of stronger, faster, more athletic guys in the NBA—especially defenders—who do their best to make my life miserable out there. I could get wrapped up in or distracted by that—but that wouldn't change anything. I am my own type of basketball player. Do I wish I could just drive down the lane and dunk every play? Absolutely! But I have discovered there's something even better than that sort of natural ability.

If something is handed to you or a task comes easy, you won't get the chance to develop the drive you need to sustain excellence. I wouldn't have the confidence I have if I hadn't had people tell me I was too small to be a threat on the court. I had to develop habits of positive self-talk to encourage myself, because there were plenty of voices telling me no. I didn't look the part of a Division I recruit, but that made me work harder, maximizing my skill set as a sharpshooter who could tire out any opponent by racing all over the court.

Being real, we know that not everyone is going to make it to the top tier of every dream they pursue—just like not everyone who picks up a ball makes it to the league. But the worst way to fail is to lose what makes you different because you're busy trying to be someone you're not. **Find strength in what sets you apart.** It's your superpower.

That's one of the first pieces of advice I give to young kids: Be comfortable with who you are as a player, but relentlessly build on those strengths. That translates to everything you do throughout your life, whether it's at school, at work, or at home. Don't get fixated on what you can't do—the time you waste worrying about things you can't change is time you're not using to maximize the skills you do have.

Remember, you, exactly as you are, are here for a reason. So make the most of the time and gifts you have.

I'm still learning and relearning these lessons here with you.

It's wild how history repeats itself. My oldest daughter is starting to play sports but sometimes struggles a little bit with her confidence. When she plays volleyball, she might launch 10 great serves in a row and then miss one. The one she missed? It ruins her day.

"Hey, do you think Daddy makes all the shots that I take?" I ask her. "Did you know that I miss, too?"

She seems surprised. "Oh yeah?"

"How often do you think I miss shots in a game?"

"Like two out of ten?"

"Now, see?" I say. "It's a lot more than that. A lot."

Playing sports teaches you some hard lessons about perseverance and confidence—and one of those lessons is that success usually has a lot of failure wrapped up in it. So there's no point in being afraid to try because you're afraid to fail— **we only truly fail when we shrink away from challenges to stay in a comfort zone.**

Those are the lessons that I get to teach her now. And she teaches them back to me: Now that she's a little bit more engaged—actually watching me play—I have that lesson in the back of my mind when I'm out there playing. Let your kids see you try. Your misses taught you—they're the thing that got you here just as much as the makes—and they can teach the next generation, too.

It's tempting to look around and see people who are on different timelines—they may be older or younger or just at a different point in their development—and measure your progress by their journey. But I can't know what's brought them to that place, and, more than that, comparing myself to others will give me a false sense of superiority or inferiority, neither of which will give me the fuel I need for my own improvement.

Instead, I put the blinders on and compare myself to myself. What is the next limit I need to challenge myself to push past? I shoot a hundred threes at the end of every workout, which provides a specific measurement I can use to track my progression from day to day. It allows me to be my own accountability partner.

Feelings are important, but data is something you can measure. What stat can you track in your own life to make yourself accountable for your own progress?

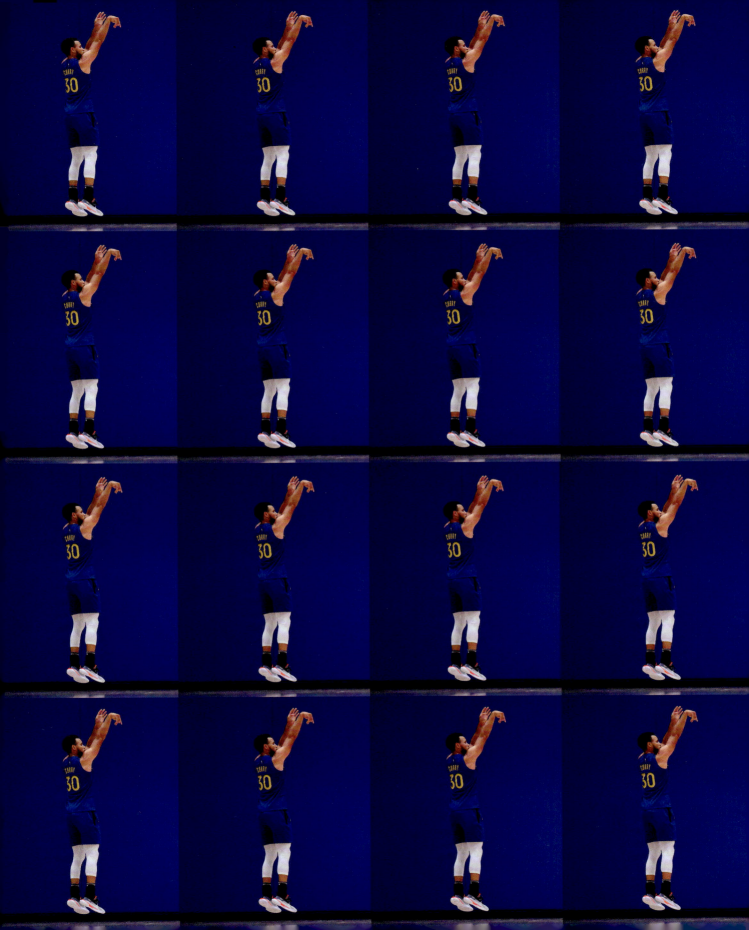

From a technical standpoint, **the greatest shooters all rely on one thing: consistency in their release point.**

The release point is the exact height and position of your shooting hand as the ball leaves it. The best players develop the ability to repeat the same release every single time.

If you looked at photos of all the thousands of shots I took this season, the top quadrant of every photo—the ball leaving my hand—would look exactly the same. Doesn't matter if I'm shooting two feet from the rim or from the logo, releasing a pull-up jumper in transition with seconds left on the clock or getting shots up in my backyard court with my dogs in the middle of the night. It's the same shot, every time, no matter what.

The times wh
uncomfort
inflection poi
The discomf
know you a

n you're most
ble are the
ts in your life.
rt is how you
e changing.

It was my dad who taught me to pay attention to the release point in other players' shots and be conscious of it in mine. Once you have that fixed and precise, you can be creative with everything else. No matter where and when you shoot, you never have to ask, "Is this a good shot?" because the shot has all the technical components of one. That makes the question more dynamic: "Is this a good shot *now*?" If I don't have to think about my shot, my mind is free to answer that second question—I can watch where a defender is moving, spot where my teammates are on the floor, and reflect on the game situation. **Having a fixed form unleashes my creativity in every other part of the game.**

Even if you understand the importance of consistency, sometimes you'll fall out of sync: The ball starts flying a little bit to the left or the right. Somewhere your mechanics have come undone.

Say my shot is coming out flat. I know the problem is either that I'm not getting enough spin on it when I release it or my arm angle is too flat.

If the shot is coming up short, the answer is obvious: I'm not getting enough power from my feet. Most times, that means my feet have gotten too spaced out when I'm taking my shot. I need to have that base underneath me. Misalignment happens to all shooters, but **the best ones don't panic.** They quickly recalibrate.

The moment of decision came on the heels of my parents racing around town to get me to baseball and basketball tournaments the same weekend my freshman year of high school.

"We can't keep this pace up," my pops said.

"So, which sport do you want to invest in?" my mom asked. "Invest yourself in fully?"

It didn't take long. When I thought about what I actually loved practicing, it was obviously basketball. When I told them, my pops nodded.

"Okay, if that's what your choice is," he said, "your shot needs to change."

My mom agreed. Sonya Curry had been a star athlete; she knew what it took.

"You're a great shooter," my dad said. "In fact, you need to shoot more. But with your mechanics, you might struggle transitioning to varsity because you're undersized."

Now I nodded. I'd been willing myself to grow for years, without luck, so this was not news to me.

"Your low release point means your shots can get blocked. It's going to be really hard for you to create enough space to get your shot off with those mechanics."

I cleared my throat. "Yeah."

"If you want to be successful at the next level," he continued, "you should consider spending this summer trying to get your release point higher." It would be extremely hard work, he told me, and I nodded like I knew what that meant. "You're gonna have to break your shot down to the studs," he said. "You don't have to, but we'll support you if you do because we think it will help you be successful not just in school, but at the next level after that."

"We're not gonna do this for you," my mom said. "But we'll give you the tools you need to figure it out."

The choice was mine. And I wanted it. But I didn't know what I was signing up for.

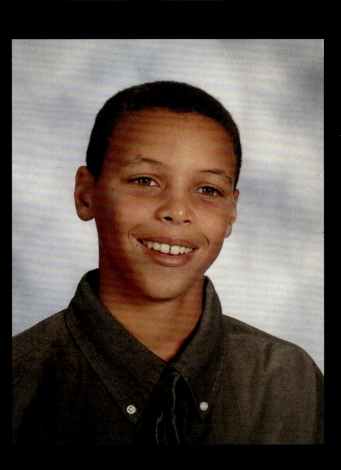

We had a three-quarter court in our backyard surrounded by white stucco walls with a Spalding rim on either side. The asphalt of the court would just collect the summer heat all day. I was going to be out there six days a week, two sessions a day.

The work was to remake my technique through form shooting. (Form shooting is just what it sounds like: shooting drills that focus exclusively on form.) I would start my shooting motion, but right before my usual catapult release, I'd stop and slowly raise my arms. I'd do that same movement, in slow motion, over and over and over again.

My dad had trained himself to be a great shooter in high school, when his coach gave him the key to his barn, which had a beat-up floor and a basket. Hours and hours, rain or snow, cold or hot. He knew not to rush the process. The average kid's temptation might be to make a couple of shots in the paint and quickly move to the three-point line. But he taught me that you have to rigorously train your body in the proper form on close shots before you move out to the arc. **The repetition is how you lock in your mechanics.** This is where I learned—not intellectually, but in my body—that consistency at the point of release is the key to great shooting.

"I don't care if you make a hundred in a row from two feet," my dad said. "That's all we're shooting." And then he'd go inside. The next day, same thing. This would go on until he saw that the integrity of my shot mechanics was consistent. Then I could start to work my way out. But even then, I moved farther back at painfully small increments.

For three months I didn't shoot outside the paint. The high-school three-point line, this thing I thought I was working

toward, seemed a light-year away.

It was *hard*. Proper technique can be physically draining when you're first learning it. My arms were sore from working muscles I hadn't even known I had. I was finding my new release point in slow motion, mapping over my old muscle memory and retraining my body with a new pattern that I could repeat without thought.

It was a lesson in maintaining commitment without immediate validation. I was used to thinking that my value as a player was measured in makes. In being fast enough and smart enough to slip past a defender. Now I was learning that my value was in the work I was willing to do to get better—and in the patience I could summon to do that work slowly, carefully, and consistently, before it ever started to pay me back.

Every morning, my parents would come out to start the session, then leave me alone. They wanted to see how my work ethic developed. My younger brother Seth was around, but in his own world at the other hoop, making all kinds of moves, shooting from all over the place. I was envious that he could just enjoy basketball. Meanwhile, I was down on my end legit struggling just to get to the point where I could shoot outside the paint.

In retrospect, having Seth there was helpful. It was comforting to know I had a partner in crime putting in the hours, even if we were on two separate channels. But I would also sometimes glance over at Seth, watch him moving around with such joy and abandon, and be reminded that basketball was *fun*. I'd see him and think, *That's where I was and where I'm trying to go.*

Whenever you're trying to develop a skill, there will be moments when you wonder: *Am I actually getting better? Is this worth it?*

In investing, they talk about the J-curve. Imagine a big J on a page: The dip at the start of the letter is when you're investing in something but haven't gotten any returns yet, and then the line rises, and fast. **Whatever the investment is, you're going to get feedback on the loss quicker than you get any positive returns**—it takes longer for the trajectory to start shooting up. When you're in that down phase, you have no idea how far it's going to go until it starts to go the other way.

This is trouble if you're motivated solely by the validation of quick results. You'll give up if you are results-focused instead of process-focused, because working harder doesn't make that curve go up faster.

There's no avoiding the dip, so you have to survive it. You need to find a way to manage your emotions during the down curve, stick with the process, and trust that it's going to lead you to your goal.

During that summer, while I was still in the middle of remaking my shot, I briefly had to leave my isolation and return to the world. I had committed to go to my school's basketball camps, and I couldn't tell them, "I'm still working on my shot," and bail out. I had to play.

I was one of the worst players at the camps. I had lost my old identity as a shooter—the kid who could catapult from deep—and I had no confidence yet in my new style. I didn't know who I was on the court, the place where I'd always felt most at home.

This guy Damier Pitts, who would later be highly recruited, had transferred to our school. We knew each other a little bit but he'd never seen me play. He just knew me as Dell Curry's son and someone who was supposed to be next up for Charlotte Christian basketball. The first time we played together, I didn't make a shot outside the paint the entire game.

I'm sure he was thinking, "This what I signed up for? To play with *him*?" I'm sure he was thinking that because he actually said it out loud. I was able to laugh it off, but **in that moment I just felt lost.**

I loved basketball so much. When you love something with such passion and want to succeed at it, you take it as a matter of faith that devoting all your time and energy to it will yield results. But nothing was working. I'd relied on putting the ball in the basket for my confidence and identity. Now I thought I just might miss forever.

I didn't see any progress until that November, when my high-school team was getting into our preseason work.

Aside from camp and my little brother, up to that point I had been working in isolation, just me, the basketball, and the hoop. There was no defense to react to, no gameplay whatsoever.

Being with my teammates again helped—feeling the joy and the stakes of real competition. At home, I was still putting in the same work, but now that I could integrate what I was learning at home into my game, I had a truer understanding of what I was doing and why it was worth it.

There wasn't some moment where things just clicked and my shots started dropping. It was a gradual process, but over time, I began to sense that I was on the upward slope of the curve. I started putting the ball in the basket again—not always, but enough to give me the confidence to take more chances.

By the time I was done, my shot, now broken down and rebuilt, was essentially the same as my shot today. I was not as strong I am now, so my release point was a little lower. But **the basic structure of the shot was there.**

I sometimes wonder: What would I tell that 13-year-old out there practicing alone for months? The cliché would be to say, *Stick with it. You do this now, you'll be set*. But no, that's not what I'd say.

First, I would acknowledge to young me that this summer will be one of the hardest tasks I'd ever face in my basketball life: breaking down the one thing I thought I did well to try to do it better, while feeling so far away from what I hoped the end result would be.

And this is the advice I would give myself: This may seem like it's as hard as it gets, but you're going to have to do variations of this same work a hundred more times in your life. Different scenarios and settings. Different challenges. But the same hard work with the same distant and uncertain outcome. There will be injuries to come back from and seasons where your team just doesn't win. And as time goes by, the challenges will be less about basketball and more about the stuff of life. You're going to have to bring this same energy, focus, attentiveness, and perseverance to each one of those episodes. But that's what you're learning now. **This pain will reward you for the rest of your life.**

My son Canon's got a hoop on his wall, and he's been testing his range a little bit. I try to give him some pointers on how to shoot, but he won't listen. "No," he'll tell me, "this is how I'm doing it." I respect that. **You can only listen when you're ready.**

A couple of years back, I had a two-month shooting slump. Some players are afraid of that word, but you have to call things what they are if you want to fix them. And I was *slumping*.

There were lots of articles about it in the press because it's an easy subject for a quick column. They would just write about their pet theories: I was getting older, it was mid-season fatigue from overtraining, I was unhappy with the team. It wasn't any of those things, by the way, but I stopped reading the articles anyway. While missing shots is a great way to learn, **obsessing over failure is just a distraction from the work of improvement.** So whenever I hit a slump, I fall back on a practice that helps me stay focused: *amnesia*.

In the context of a game, amnesia means forgetting my last shot as soon as I run back up the court, whether it's a make or miss. There are times, of course, when you miss a shot and want to figure out what's wrong right away, correct it, and quickly recalibrate, all in the flow of the game. But for deeper problems, it's better to save your worry for practice and between the games.

As a shooter, what I need is confidence that the *next* shot is going to go in. To maintain that confidence—and to stay in the calm flow state I work so hard to achieve—my job is to *not* overanalyze.

That applies to so much of life. You let a little bit of doubt creep in while you're performing, and soon it infects your whole process. Doubt and worry will sap you of the juice and energy you need to perform in the moment.

When I was in that slump that seemed never-ending, I went to the practice gym alone between games. There I had the quiet and time to analyze the movement of my body as I shot. In that environment, shooting the ball is almost a form of meditation—I took that time to let everything else fall away and just inhabited my body as fully as I could, making myself aware of every subtle movement. And in that meditative state, the answer came to me: The problem was at the bottom of my feet. I was starting my shooting sequence wrong, leaning on my toes just slightly and not focusing on driving the ground down with the balls of my feet. Because the shot rises from the ground, that slight difference distorted the rest of my shooting motion, so that by the time the motion got to my release, I wasn't shooting the ball. I was throwing it.

    I adjusted on my next shot. The ball went in.

    "Oh," I whispered to myself. I went up for another shot. The ball went in again. And again. Then they had to find something else to write about. The slump was over.

It's harder now for young players to keep blinders on and stay focused when social media is there to remind you of your every make and miss—and everyone else's. You might see people posting their wins and want to do the same. You might even look at me and other people who've made it to the bright stage of the NCAA, the NBA, or the WNBA and feel a twinge of envy. But just remember that all you'll see in the media is a product, not a process. This whole book is meant to reveal all the steps along the way—the bumps and hurdles, the misses and mistakes that make us. **No one is made of wins.**

When you're coming up, **try to find the toughest people you can to play against.** The best in your city or field. Even when they beat you, you'll learn something. When your opponents are too close to your level, you're living off crumbs of competition. You can't grow on that.

By my junior year of high school, Seth and I were always out looking for pickup games. Mostly, we'd wind up at the YMCA in the suburbs of Charlotte, the Siskey Y. We thought that's where the best runs were.

One day we decided to try out a different gym—the Harris Y, downtown, closer to Charlotte's Center City. That's when we discovered that we'd only scratched the surface of the local competition. Harris made Siskey look like a church league. Some guys who played overseas would come to Harris to work out, or people like Alan Anderson, a young guy who was with the Charlotte Bobcats at the time.

It was the most fun I've ever had getting beat. "Alright," I'd think to myself, rising up off the court from getting knocked down again. "*This* is the level I need to be at."

Anderson would be out there talking trash in his raspy, fed-up voice. "Y'all have been going over to the Siskey Y," he told us, "but you have not been over *here*." This was a basketball culture I'd never really seen before. The vibe was kill or be killed.

But we did manage to beat Anderson's team one game. He started demanding a rematch before he would leave. His team won the rematch, of course, and as he grabbed his backpack to go, he was still trash-talking us on the way out the door. "You're only as good as your last game! You're only as good as your last game!"

It was beautiful. In two hours, I learned lessons that would carry me through the next years: **what it feels like to get challenged and exposed, what you learn in defeat, the thrill of getting outside your comfort zone, and the value of playing against the best.**

We were looking for some runs, but I found something better: a new approach to the game.

I went to an AAU tournament in Las Vegas the summer before my senior year at Charlotte Christian. I played in front of all these college coaches, thinking, **Okay, this is my time.** After the tournament, I thought my parents would soon be telling me about all the people calling with offers, but there was nothing. I watched people I played against, guys I knew I could beat, get recruiting letters and scholarship offers. I just didn't pass the eye test—I was 5'9" my junior year; a growth spurt brought me to six feet as a senior.

    I ended up playing college ball at Davidson College, and in my sophomore year I led our school of 1,700 students into the Elite Eight. We were a mid-major making a run to the Final Four, and we came heartbreakingly close. One missed three-pointer away. Right after the game, with everyone crying in the locker room, a reporter asked me if I was about to declare for the NBA draft.

    It was the furthest thing from my mind in that moment of loss, but then the realization hit me that the NBA was the next step. To make myself a more valuable draft pick, I had to add to my game, and in my junior year I started the transition from the shooting guard position to point guard. In the NBA, shooting guards average about two inches taller than point guards. Plus, I needed to be a more formidable playmaker and scorer. College had been an adventure—and it's an adventure I've described in detail before, so I won't repeat it all here—but new challenges awaited me.

The draft process is wild. No matter how much my agent, Jeff Austin, assured me that everything was in place for my pick, a new narrative emerged every day. Before the draft, Jeff ran me through a circuit of pre-draft meetings and workouts. I worked out for four teams—Charlotte, Washington, Sacramento, and New York.

The Knicks coach, Mike D'Antoni, talked to me about my future role on the team and laid out the squad he hoped to run with me, including the young Italian prospect Danilo Gallinari and my future teammate David Lee. I'd be the point guard of what D'Antoni envisioned as a remake of his successful, high-scoring Phoenix Suns teams, with me in the Steve Nash role. It was such a certainty that the Knicks would go for me with their number-eight pick that D'Antoni made a joke of it.

Less than two weeks before NBA Draft Night, he walked up to me at the end of my practice at the Knicks training facility in Greenburgh, New York.

"We can't draft you," he said, frowning.

"Oh, why?" I asked, dying a little.

"Because Allan Houston doesn't want to be the second-best shooter in Knicks history," he said, laughing. Allan's nine years as a Knick had ended in 2005. That was the confidence he had in my future as a Knick. **And I was ready for it, too.**

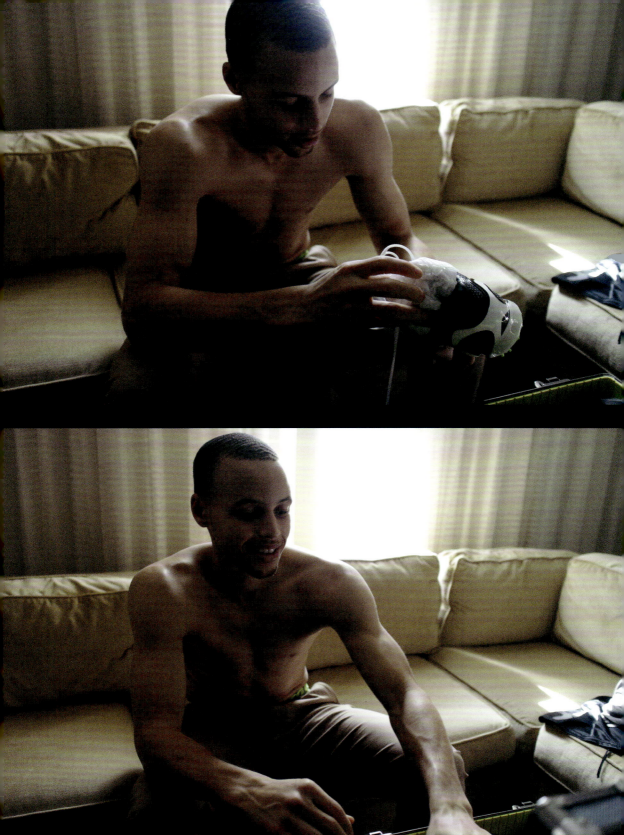

My conversations with Golden State were different, in that they were nonexistent.

Golden State had the number-seven pick, just ahead of the Knicks, but they thought it would be crazy to take a player they hadn't worked out, and my father assured me they wouldn't. I figured he was talking from experience, but what I didn't know was that **he and my agent had explicitly told Golden State not to draft me.** They were aware of some organizational dysfunction the Warriors were going through, and they wanted to steer me clear of it. Unbeknownst to me, Don Nelson had called my dad the day of the draft and asked, "What's your feelings toward us drafting your son?" My dad later told me what his immediate answer was. "Don't. You asked me the question; I'll tell you the truth. Don't."

It was time for the draft to begin. Each team gets three minutes to give their pick to the league commissioner, who announces it to the assembled crowd of players, parents, and local fans. I was at my table with my parents, my sister Sydel, and my girlfriend Ayesha. I am blessed that Ayesha Curry is now my wife, but back then she was Ayesha Alexander, the most beautiful girl I'd ever seen ever since we first met at church when we were 14. The truth is, I could barely look at her at that Wednesday-night church youth group because she was, and is, *so* stunning. She'd grown up in Toronto, and we bonded over memories of the candy you could only get in Canada.

And now we were all watching as NBA commissioner David Stern came to the podium and announced the number-one pick: "With the first pick in the 2009 NBA draft, the Los Angeles Clippers select Blake Griffin." Next, Memphis picked seven-footer Hasheem Thabeet. Now the selections moved from bigs to smaller guards like me. James Harden went third, Tyreke Evans fourth. I started to feel foolish that I had been worried I'd go early and lose my chance to be picked by the Knicks. Washington had traded their pick to Minnesota, giving the Timberwolves the fifth and sixth picks. My whole table was stock-still, willing Minnesota to skip me. *Just get through these two,* I told myself. *And then it's guaranteed that I'm going to New York.* Only Golden State stood between me and the Knicks—but there was no way *they'd* pick me.

When Minnesota took two point guards—Ricky Rubio and Jonny Flynn—I felt a flash of annoyance. **Four straight point guards over me?**

Golden State was next up. They were clearly thinking hard about something because they let the selection clock run down to zero. Finally, Commissioner Stern returned to the podium. "With the seventh pick in the 2009 NBA draft, the Golden State Warriors select . . ."

Stern said my name.

My immediate thought was: *But I ain't even talked to them.*

I'd never heard boos like that before. It was a New York crowd full of Knicks fans, and they'd been sold the same narrative I had: that I was going to leave the Garden that night a Knick.

Coach Nelson had other plans. Golden State had planned to pick Blake Griffin, but when he went first and Minnesota didn't take me, everything changed for them. I would be on the first flight in the morning to Oakland, which felt like the farthest franchise on the map from my home in Charlotte.

Be open to th
Things will h
and sometime
that they're hap

unexpected.
ppen to you,
you won't see
pening *for* you.

"Golden State's not a city," my grandma told me on draft night. Everyone on the East Coast thinks California means L.A. **My mother didn't even know where in California the Warriors played.** "My baby's going so far away," she said.

I'd been to the Bay Area once. I played my last college game there against the St. Mary's Gaels that March. We'd lost. It had been a hostile crowd.

But I'd grow to love the Bay Area's fans and everything about that cluster of cities and towns in Northern California. It's still weird to think about it: how **out of nowhere a place can become your home.**

It's ironic that **the more elite the level of the game—from high school to college, to the league, to the playoffs—the more aggressive and less polished it becomes.** This feels true in every part of life. You may have noticed it yourself. As your skills bring you to higher stages, things don't get easier: You discover there's less space to move and more friction and resistance. Your opponents do more to stop you, becoming aggressive, fearful of giving up position. And even as the game gets rougher, the refs catch less and less. And when they do step in, the margin for success is so razor-thin that one bad call can change your fate.

People might tell you this ahead of time, but you don't believe it until it's happening to you. You reach the next level and suddenly you're right back to solving the old puzzle: How do I succeed *now*?

I didn't know the recent history of the Warriors, but I knew they were in what's politely called a period of transition. They were briefly a playoff team two years before I was drafted—the unforgettable "We Believe" 2006–2007 season, when the underdog Warriors made NBA history as the first number-8 seed to beat a number-1 seed in a best-of-7 playoff series. That year, Oakland fell in love again with their home team. But then a bunch of the guys the fans loved got traded for pieces that didn't make sense, so by the time I arrived there was a lot of distrust and dysfunction in the organization, from the executive suites to the locker room. In just *two years*, the culture had gone totally rotten. Maybe you've worked in a place like this.

Controlling people's feelings is an impossible task, so good leaders create a culture where feelings can be contained and altercations quickly overcome. When everyone shares a mission, issues can be solved quickly, with a collective eye on the shared goal. Effective leaders cultivate an environment of honesty and transparency; if they speak with candor about their own shortcomings, it makes it easier for everyone else to acknowledge mistakes and missteps, which allows the team to course-correct instead of letting problems linger.

When you walk into a place with a leadership void, on the other hand, you're likely to see people trying to assert what control they can in toxic ways, by gossiping, trash-talking, and backstabbing.

That was what the Warriors were dealing with. They'd gone from the unifying identity of "We Believe," us against the world, to resenting one another. I'm not just talking about the players; the whole organization suffered from a culture of mistrust.

And now here I was, a bright-eyed 21-year-old rookie from a tiny Christian college, strolling into training camp as naïve as they come.

Before my rookie season began, I played for the Warriors' summer-league team in Las Vegas. When I got there, I knew only one guy on the squad: Anthony Morrow, who I grew up with in Charlotte. He'd played for the Warriors the year before and I knew he was trying to make his way back onto the team. C. J. Watson, who'd played college basketball for the Tennessee Volunteers, was also there trying to prove himself after Coach Nelson brought him up from the D-league with two back-to-back 10-day contracts the year before. C.J. and A.Mo kind of gave me the lay of the land on how chaotic the organization was, but also **how much fun it was to play in Coach Nelson's system.**

"Nellie's gonna show up five minutes before practice," C.J. said. "He's gonna set a chair down right on the sideline and after we warm up, he's going to call plays."

A.Mo finished for him: "And then you're just gonna hoop."

"That's the practice plan?"

"Yeah," they said together, smiling.

At my first training camp, that's exactly what happened. We did a little bit of skill work just to get warmed up. And then out came the chair, placed on the sideline by an assistant, followed shortly by Nellie himself, 6'6" and 69 years old, who sat down. I noticed he had a whistle in his hand. Then, in that Midwestern twang of his, he started calling out plays—"Four side!" "One side!" "Two side!"—and we'd run them. He would yell at people who didn't play fast enough or turned down a shot. "Nellie Ball" was Coach's invention, a style of run-and-gun offense relying on speed, but with not much use for even the fundamentals of defense. The system is sometimes called "small ball," but it was really designed for Coach Nelson to spread the floor with all his best players at once, regardless of their traditional positions, and get the ball in the basket as quickly as possible. Through all of training camp, we might have done maybe one defensive drill. That's one criticism of Nellie Ball—that its heavy emphasis on offense, and the seeming chaos of players coming in and out of the game at random, hurts a team's defensive fundamentals.

I had to laugh when Coach Nelson recently told ESPN that the strategy was really just about working with what you have. "You only play Nellie Ball when you don't have a very good team, or when you have a bunch of good small players and not many good big players," he said. "When you have bad teams, you've got to be creative to win games you're not supposed to win." So **maybe we were just a bad team.**

Nellie Ball expanded my offensive horizons, but its key requirement—shooting quickly and outrunning opponents—had always been my thing. Now it was, at Coach's insistence, everyone else on the team's thing, too. On a run-and-gun team, I wasn't sure how to distinguish myself.

It's not bragging to embrace these little wins, and it's not prideful— I was just celebrating a turn of the J-curve. The investment was beginning to pay off.

As a rookie, you're always waiting for that moment when you feel like you actually know what you're doing. It kind of shocks you a little bit—when you do what you're supposed to do in the flow of a game—and when it does, you want desperately to hold on to the feeling. Take it home and admire it like a trophy. But more than just enjoying the dopamine hit of replaying a triumphant moment, you can use it to help you visualize future success.

I needed a moment like that at training camp, where I felt like everyone but me knew the play calls and understood the flow. Everyone else had played in NBA games and was familiar with the league's elevated speed and physicality. I was trying to figure it out on the fly.

But the moment I'd been hoping for finally came. I can remember it as if I'm driving home from that practice right now. We were playing on the left wing of the practice court in Oakland. My team was running down the court in transition when our star guard Monta Ellis threw the ball ahead to me.

Nellie was always a proponent of a very specific approach to transition plays—he believed in creating a wave of momentum by making quick decisions and eating up any space the defense gives. The theory is that if you let the defense reset and slow your pace, you lose the advantage. It sounds simple, but it's not always easy to pull off.

I caught Monta's pass, brought the ball down to dribble, and picked a spot for penetration. Standing in front of me on defense was Kelenna Azubuike, a big, strong 6'5" defender. In a blink, I crossed him over and watched as he kept going one way and I went the other. Now free, I pulled up for a short jumper. *Swish*.

I was euphoric, but I knew I had to stay cool, which was hard because in my head I was losing it. But I had to compose myself—I didn't want anyone else to see how giddy I was and become the rookie joke for the rest of practice. But my boy who lived with me my rookie year, Chris Strachan, he'll tell you: It was the first thing I told him when I burst into our apartment after practice. "Yo, you won't believe what happened today."

I got the film and everything, but I had to camouflage how thirsty I was. I told the coach who ran film, "Hey, can I get the film from practice so I can review some play calls?"

But you and I know why I got that film: I needed to watch that crossover again. And again and again. I wanted to hold on to that moment.

I watched Monta Ellis during our practices. He hadn't said a word to me, but his talent spoke volumes. **Monta was a naturally gifted player with a singular drive.** He was drafted by the Warriors right out of his Jackson, Mississippi, high school in 2005 and played every game with a mercenary's mindset. No matter how much chaos there was in the organization, his attitude was "Give me the ball and I'll get you a bucket." He had helped build the team's "We Believe" success without getting much credit in the press. Nellie didn't help, calling him "difficult to coach."

Monta was a 6'3" guard like me, so he didn't exactly welcome my arrival. At our preseason media day that year, he offered the press his opinion that you can't play two small guys in the backcourt. The comment had some merit. It *is* hard to play two small guards in the backcourt. But the delivery and the timing—and the fact that I had not yet had a single conversation with him—well, that *was* a little weird. And it gave the media a narrative to run with.

Here's the thing: Monta was already a veteran at 24. He had practically been forced into a leadership role on a team that didn't otherwise have an identity. Monta was still growing into the veteran presence he would soon fully assume. I learned a lot watching him grow into that role and would be grateful for it later. But forget leadership for a second—what I remember most about him that first year was the joy of playing basketball with someone like the Mississippi Bullet. The way he put pressure on defenses, blowing by the man guarding him and finishing from every angle? It was a master class in the speed of the NBA. I loved every second of it.

We had our first preseason game October 4 against the Clippers. My drive to Oracle was nerve-racking. Even having been around that environment growing up—and having visualized this moment since I was a kid—it still felt like an out-of-body experience. I couldn't believe it was actually happening.

And then I didn't play the whole first quarter.

That's because Nellie used what he called the "hockey sub" rotation pattern in the preseason—all five players on the court were substituted out at the same time. So, I only played the second and fourth quarters. Spending the first 12 minutes just sitting there watching helped calm my nerves a little bit. Then I looked behind me at one point in the first quarter. Oracle Arena was half-full. Not a good omen.

We won, by the way, with a score of 108–101. I got five points, making two of nine shots. **"He doesn't look like it, but he has quick hands and quick feet,"** Nellie told reporters about me after. "He's going to be a special player someday." But not today, apparently.

When you meet a new coach or manager, you want to show that you can be coached. Yes, they have to earn your trust, too, but they need to know that you're not going to waste their time. They will test you early, giving you specific instructions to see how much you're listening and processing. If you can't do that in a pregame or interview situation, you're not going to be able to perform when it matters.

Some of this coaching is going to take the form of criticism. But always remember, you put yourself out there to get that guidance—to be exposed so that you can improve.

Don't cower from the criticism. If it's right, take it to heart. **If it's wrong, prove it.**

I still get butterflies and nerves before every game. Regular season, preseason, Game 7 of the Finals, it doesn't matter. I understand now that I can't stop this great wave of nerves from coming before games, but I can control them once they get here.

I have a simple method—you can do it with me now: Take a couple deep breaths. Do it with intention, really slowing yourself down. Let your mind set the tone for your body, don't let your body set the tone for your mind.

Breathing is the meeting point for the physical and mental aspects of my game. It's a practice I carry from training sessions to preseason camp to the heart of the season to the playoffs and beyond.

I teach this simple breathing routine to young people at our basketball camps because I know their energy levels can sometimes outrun their oxygen levels. They just want to hoop and barely need to warm up, let alone pay attention to their breathing while playing. But learning deep and intentional breathing will not just calm their nerves; it will help them process information better and respond faster.

Keep this in mind the next time you get your own version of pregame butterflies before some important task or project. Take note of whatever it is that gets those butterflies going and then intentionally slow and deepen your breathing. If you have time, do this short breathing exercise at the start of the day, because as soon as you wake up, your body's nervous system is going to be trying to speed up your mind and have you processing information a lot faster than you need to—which can lead to mistakes. Even if the task is your version of Game 7, where you throw everything you have out there to get a win, you should remind your body that it's just another day. So breathe.

Don't be afraid of the butterflies or wish them away. They are there because something matters to you. You never want that feeling to stop.

Five days after my first preseason game, Nellie was still doing the same thing—making me sit out the first quarter—but I didn't mind: I spent those 12 minutes watching Kobe Bryant play up close at the Forum in L.A.

In the second quarter I was finally on the court playing defense. He wasn't my matchup, but Kob and me got cross-matched on this one possession. He's trying to post me up when I hear him hissing for the ball. *Sssssss.* The sound of a mamba before it strikes.

Holy— I think. *What? That's a real thing?* I'm trying to guard him, but he's getting deeper into position. Even as I'm trying to bump and get physical, he backs me all the way down into the paint.

Sssss. As he's calling for the ball with his right hand, he slaps his other hand on my calf, fingers splayed in a grip pointing down to my ankle. I'm trying but I literally cannot move. I know this is a foul, so I'm looking at the ref, who's just standing there watching. I yell at the ref—"Yo, yo, yo!"—but he just stares at me. Kob keeps his hand locked around my leg through it all. I notice the slightest, slightest smile on his face.

Finally, he gets the ball and jab-steps and spins baseline, then finishes at the rim. He doesn't look back at me as he's running back down the court. I was watching it from outside my body, my mind offering commentary on the action. First, *Yo, this is really happening,* then, *Oh, he's beating me,* and then a deep feeling of embarrassment that I was the rookie complaining to the refs, trying to get a foul called in a preseason game.

It *was* just preseason, but I could already feel the higher level of physicality and intensity of the professional game. **I can't imagine a quicker education in the game than having to guard Kobe for that one possession.** Welcome to the NBA.

Nobody thought I should start the first game of the regular season, but that may have been a product of our dysfunctional team politics. I'd played pretty well toward the end of preseason, so I felt I'd earned it. Coach Nelson did, too. It made me uncomfortable knowing I was the new guy getting that opportunity over some players with more seniority, but I tried to enjoy the moment.

I believe in choosing happiness. I couldn't control how it made other people feel that I got the starting nod. But I could choose to just let it make me happy.

There was a space at Oracle next to our locker room where a full-time chaplain held a 15- to 20-minute service before games. Before that first regular-season game, the service was attended by me, three more Warriors, and two guys from the Rockets.

Today, **I still make sure to take a moment with the Word before every game.**

Playing for a purpose is as natural and necessary to me as breathing. Right before my first practice in college, my mom texted me her favorite Bible verse. It was Romans 8:28, "All things work together for the good of those who love Him and are called according to His purpose." To this day, I lean on that verse whenever I feel challenged. That verse beautifully describes the faith that drives me but also conveys a powerful sense of acceptance, to live with whatever comes. When I let go of the ball, I have confidence and faith that it's going to work out in my favor. That doesn't mean it will always go in. It means that there's a reason for whatever the outcome is. You can control what you can control, but beyond you is another force directing everything. In the end, things will be the way they're supposed to be.

I'm not a guy who bashes people over the head with a Bible. I love to talk about my faith, I take every opportunity I get, but I also let my actions speak for themselves. Before I am a basketball player, I am a husband and a father. And before all those things, I am a believer, because that is the root of everything I do. So, to know me and the way that I play is to know where my inspiration and foundation come from.

Ever since that first game at Oracle, I've made a habit of digging into the Word in our little locker-room chapel before games. It's a reminder of my purpose. And there's always gratitude in that room, too—a spirit that we are obligated to do right by the blessings we've been given.

Twice as a rookie, I got to play Allen Iverson. Once when he was with the Memphis Grizzlies, then two months later when he was back with the 76ers for his second Philly run. It was his fourteenth and last season in the league. And he cooked me.

A.I., this six-foot-tall lethal shooter, was one of my favorite point guards growing up. I modeled a lot of my ball-handling on him. Or tried to. I always made an effort to play it cool when I met these greats who I'd studied on the court. I told myself to separate my fandom from the job, because now I'm not watching them—we're going at each other. But I couldn't entirely suppress the feeling of *wow*. I was on the same court as *A.I.* No, more than that, I would be responsible for checking *A.I.* when we matched up.

I knew how to guard him, or I thought I did, because I'd played against him in my head so many times as a kid. But he cooked me. A.I. didn't just change the game when he came into the league—he kept evolving, too.

Over the years, A.I. has reciprocated some of the love I have for him. He once put me in his all-time starting five on a television show. **I have that clip saved on my phone.**

I think about my first encounter with A.I.—me a rookie, him in his last years—all the time, now that I'm the veteran playing against rookies. They grew up studying my moves to the point that I sometimes feel like I'm playing in a mirror, so I have to come up with new things, just like A.I. did.

And then I cook 'em.

We lost that opening-night game to the Rockets. And then the next game to the Phoenix Suns. We stole one win after that before dropping two more.

One thing I was learning is that **team chemistry takes time to build.** Everyone knows chemistry is important to winning, so it's natural to feel a sense of urgency about expediting that bond, especially when you're losing. But the deepest chemistry forms naturally as a group of people find connection while riding a wave together.

Some measure of chemistry comes from having a shared purpose as a group, but sometimes chemistry develops from experiencing moments of adversity together. Watch your teammates when obstacles arise for them. Those can be the moments that reveal and unlock their next level of potential. Watching that happen connects you to their journey.

That intangible feeling of connection creates results on the court. It allows you to assess risks in a split second. If I turn down this shot, can I count on my teammate to make the right play? We talk about studying and respecting our opponents in order to win, but what about our teammates? Knowing who you're working with and appreciating their strengths will be key to being able to lead and delegate down the line.

It was our first road trip. We were in Indiana and had just lost to the Pacers by 14 points. After the game, seven of us got together for dinner at a local steakhouse. In the middle of the meal, Stephen Jackson called a reporter, Marc Spears, on his cell phone. While we all sat listening, Jackson started to ream Marc about a story he'd written with quotes from unnamed players saying the Warriors were tired of the daily drama over when he was getting traded, and it was particularly affecting the young roster. Oh, Stack Jack put him on speaker phone and cussed him out. We were all riveted sitting there listening because Jackson was so passionate. I also realized that I had unwittingly taken part in the "rumor mill" in the locker room. My eyes were opened a little wider—even growing up with my dad, I never saw this side of the game, the locker-room dynamics and conflicts with the media.

Stack Jack made his point clear: Don't believe it until you hear it from me. "When I know what I know, I'm gonna let you know."

I started to think about what *I* wanted people to know. What they needed to hear from me. That night I got on Twitter, which was still in its early days, and typed out a tweet:

"Promise to all the Warrior fans . . . we will figure this thing out . . . if it's the last thing we do we will figure it out."

I pressed send. Looking back, it was a little presumptuous of me—I was a rookie who had no business speaking for the team. But my use of "we" was important. When you're not used to losing that much, it doesn't sit well with you. You feel an obligation— a deep desire—to just fix it. **But to turn the tide, it had to be us.**

It's neve
proving ot
wrong. I
proving yo

r about

her people

t's about

urself right.

You only attract what you put out.

So, every single day, a team has to ask itself, "Is everything we are doing geared toward winning the championship?

Is the way that we played tonight going to lead to success in the playoffs?" That is the standard by which you have to measure yourself every day if your objective is to be a champion. Putting out excellence attracts success.

There is something beautiful about holding yourself accountable to the ultimate standard.

Coach Nelson benched me for a series of games, giving me fewer minutes with no explanation. I was trying to come into my own as an NBA player, but I went from 30 minutes or so down to 12 minutes a game.

In New York, Coach gave me one minute and five seconds before taking me out. Near the end of that brutal game, even the Knicks fans were chanting for Nellie to put me in. He finally relented by letting me play the last 1:30 of the game. It was bittersweet: I wanted to matter enough to get a chant going, but I needed to do more than dribble out the clock. I wanted meaningful minutes.

I thought about all those bench minutes recently when a younger player asked me for advice. He was worried about staying in shape while riding the bench and waiting for the call. I gave him five or six conditioning drills, things he could do to keep his skill set sharp and get his wind right. But he had the right attitude.

You only really learn patience because you're forced to. When you're not getting enough minutes (and nobody thinks they get enough), and you feel like you're invisible, you don't want to hear about the benefits of practicing patience. But the truth is that the waiting will make you a better player if you let it teach you.

The times that feel like you're standing still are times to get shot ready. It's just like how you get ready to shoot: You practice that shot-ready position—nose behind your toes, hips loaded, hands open—so that when the ball gets thrown to you it won't knock you off your feet.

When I was a rookie, the young point guards in the NBA vying for pole position were Jrue Holiday, Ty Lawson, Jeff Teague, Brandon Jennings, and me. I knew about Jennings—he had been one of the four best high-school guards in the nation, along with Holiday, Tyreke Evans, and Lance Stephenson, but shook things up by becoming the first American to bypass college to play in the Euroleague. Now he was back from Italy, still a year younger than me, and in my draft class. I did a couple of pre-draft workouts with him—one in Sacramento and one in Washington. He went tenth, to the Milwaukee Bucks.

    Nellie still had me coming off the bench when we played the Bucks on that first road trip. I got a little more run than usual, subbing in here and there for 26 minutes, while Jennings played 41. In the second quarter we tried to blitz him on defense. He came off a screen on the left side and hit me with a quick left-right cross down the middle. I went down on my butt and pretty much just sat there while Jennings drew a shooting foul at the rim. The third quarter is when Jennings really took off, scoring 29 points. He ended up with 55 for the game, a double-nickel, becoming the youngest NBA player ever to score 50-plus points in a game.

    Meanwhile, I was counting minutes. How was I going to show what I could do if I couldn't even play? But **I knew I was as good as or better than my peers.** I just needed time to figure it out—and time on the court.

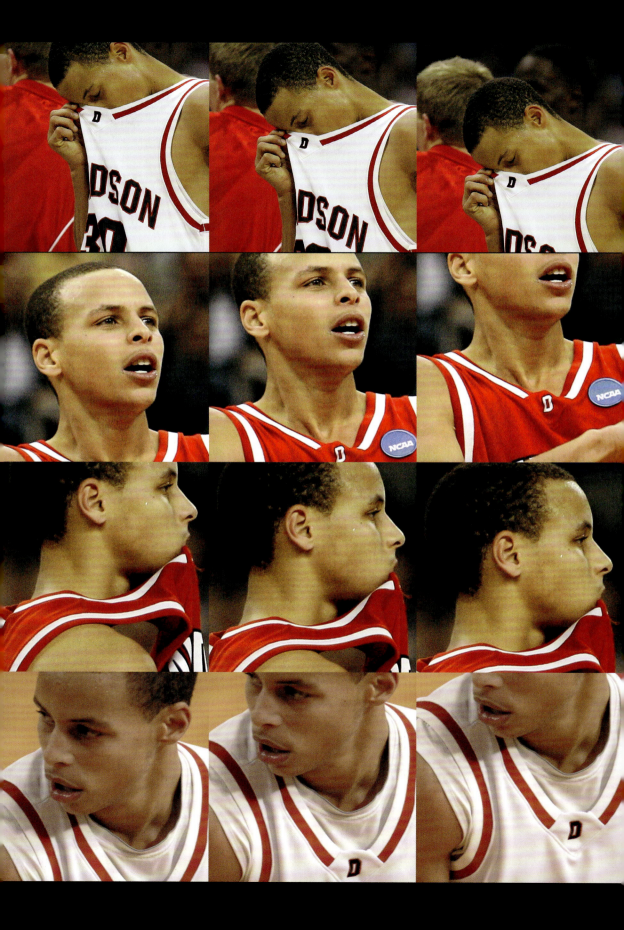

Before I left for our next game, in Cleveland, my agent had someone make a highlight reel of my college years. "Remind yourself you can play," he said.

I watched it. I recognized myself not just going through the motions on the court but shifting into a different gear— **not just in the flow, but on fire.**

I knew I *still* had that fire. I still have that fire. Sometimes we all just need a reminder. I felt that confidence coming back as we made our way to Cleveland.

I was at LeBron James's house the night before our first game in Cleveland. He was four years older than me but had six years on me in the league. Just a year and a half earlier, during my sophomore year in college, he'd come to Davidson's Sweet Sixteen game against Wisconsin at Ford Field. The future Hall of Famer, potentially the greatest of all time, gave me a jersey that day. He signed it: "To the king of basketball in North Carolina." I hung that jersey at my parents' house—that's how much it meant to me.

His house had a bowling alley in the basement, and that's where I met his son Bronny, who had just turned five—this little bulldog of a kid who was already built beyond his years. LeBron and I didn't discuss the next day's game, but I talked a little bit about what was going on with the Warriors. That was the day Stephen Jackson and Acie Law got traded. LeBron didn't say much at the time.

After our game is when he gave me his response. *After* they beat us.

Cutting his hands close to his eyes, he told me **you've got to have tunnel vision early in your career, because even if your team's not built for success, you have to find a way for you to get better.** Worry about what *you* are doing on a daily basis. Build the right habits that are gonna set *you* up for success down the road, so that when opportunities present themselves for the *team*, you're ready to walk in and meet that moment.

You've got to block out all the noise and distractions that come with losing. Just focus on getting better.

I knew this. You know this. But every now and again we need a little more motivation. He provided that in the moment, and now I hand it to you. If you're a rookie on a team, or waiting on an investor, or working with a team that isn't quite gelling, make the time productive. Figure out the player you want to be so that when the opportunity comes, you will be ready to lead.

You have to appreciate your competition. Approach them with **respect** and what I call **appropriate fear**—after all, they're coming for you. That's the only way to beat them.

Even if Coach Nelson had wanted to keep me on the bench my first year, he was running out of guys. After StackJack got traded and Monta got hurt for a little bit, the Warriors practically became a glorified G League team.

The team was not getting along, but we found something to unite around: chasing wins for Don Nelson. At 69, he had been in the league long enough that he was closing in on Lenny Wilkens's record for most regular-season wins of any coach in NBA history. The record was 1,333. We needed 24 wins that season to put him over the top. Just 24 out of 82 games.

Our streaks of losses—nine here, six there—made even that seem questionable. Adding to the stakes, it was Nellie's last season as a coach, even though he'd told reporters he'd coach the Warriors for free the next year if the owners would let him. That wasn't going to happen.

So finally, around March, **our team, a mixed bag who never had an identity, stumbled into a key ingredient of championship chemistry: a shared purpose.**

We needed to get Nellie those 24 wins.

Setbacks are there to teach us, not to define us forever. **If I give in to a losing spirit, I'll just keep finding different ways to lose.** This is true for individuals or any team you're on or leading: Absorb the lesson, but don't let the feeling linger into another game.

It was a home game the night after I turned 22. March 15. Fourth quarter, and the Lakers were beating us by 6. I came down the court with the ball, pump-faked my defender, then hit a step-back off the glass.

The camera happened to pan onto Kobe, who was on the bench, just as he leaned over to say something to Adam Morrison: "He's nice." Later I watched the footage of Kobe. First, I reacted just like a true fan. "He's talking about me." Like, what? What?

Later Kobe would remark that even though our approaches to the game were different, we each had the same willingness to do whatever it takes to win. I do it with a smile on my face and he did it with a scowl.

"There's a serious calmness about him, which is extremely deadly," Kobe told Michael Wilbon in a 2015 ESPN interview. "Because he's not up, he's not down. He's not contemplating what just happened before or worrying about what's to come next. He's just there."

I play with joy because that's who I am, but deep down I have an intense competitive fire. Behind the playfulness is a killer instinct that not many people recognize. But Kobe did.

You can exhaust your opponent.

In the first quarter, they may be physically and mentally rested. Their adrenaline is pumping, their minds coordinating well with their bodies. That's when they are most formidable.

But let's see them in the third quarter. Fourth quarter. That's what I gear all my training for these days, but unconsciously it has always been my strategy, even in high school and college: Cover ground, play on and off the ball, and stay in relentless motion for the whole game. There will always be stronger, faster guys out there who try to make my life miserable. But I try to counter that with never staying in the same spot for more than a second.

That's why I needed more minutes.

It was a little surprising how well it worked. I came into the league believing that everyone would be at a high level of conditioning. But they're not. Some people are just coasting on the thing that has always worked for them—an advantage in talent or size or athleticism.

The point of conditioning is that it allows you to do whatever your best thing is all the time, not just in short bursts. Some people can procrastinate and then summon superhuman focus "when it counts" because of a deadline. But I believe it always "counts."

It's much better—in four quarters and the across the long run of your career—to train yourself for a consistent level of energy and effort.

Condition yourself to be relentless.

The season was coming down to the wire. We beat the Raptors in Toronto on April 4, which brought Nellie into a tie for the record, but then we promptly lost to the Washington Wizards, a team with a record almost as bad as ours.

We were in Minnesota when we finally got the last win Nellie needed. Don Nelson was now the winningest coach in the NBA. We had a celebration right after the game, water pouring on everybody's heads in the middle of April, at a time when we were four games away from finishing the season 26-56.

I don't know what we would have done if we didn't have that shared purpose. **But you can push through even in the bleakest situations if you have something bigger than yourself to fight for.**

Confidence is the ultimate tool for unlocking potential. Toward the end of that first season, I felt mine growing. I'd had time on the court playing against some of the better teams in the league and some of the league's greatest players. And I'd held my own.

I see the same thing watching the next generation coming up. Once players get over that first hump of insecurity and prove themselves *to* themselves, they start to see the game—and themselves—differently. For example, look at Trae Young's second year. In a couple of games, he goes crazy in the fourth quarter, hits crucial shots, and carries his team to wins. Now he knows he can perform at a high level on the biggest stage with high stakes and in that moment he becomes a true professional, not an amateur or a tentative rookie. A player who makes that transition is different from that point on—you can just play the game, knowing that you're not trying to prove anything. The only acknowledgment you need is *results*.

Once you have a couple of those moments—surges of sudden growth where you almost shock yourself—confidence blossoms. You've unlocked the cheat code to elevate yourself to the next level.

You can be so busy trying to absorb lessons early in your career that you don't realize it when you start to meet the moment. One day you walk onto the court, and you feel like you belong. You're no longer struggling for answers and hoping for the best. **Now you believe.** You're *supposed* to be successful.

By the end of the season, I had learned that my skills—shooting the ball well and playing with finesse—could translate to the NBA. But I could also see the necessary next steps ahead of me, the progression of things I'd have to do to improve.

I needed to get stronger. I was still pretty skinny, which created a problem mostly on the defensive end, where I struggled to hold my ground against bigger guys, but it was affecting my offensive game, too. Any time I got in the lane, I would be pushed and knocked off-balance, which made it harder to make the right pass or finish at the rim.

As a player you have to constantly evolve. Even phenoms in the league, endowed with gifts you can't really teach—size or athleticism—have to evolve to stay relevant: Seven-footers have to learn to shoot threes, a player with a jaw-dropping vertical leap needs to see the floor better. For the rest of us, evolution is even more important. The game changes as the level of competition rises, and the role you played on the way up might not be the role you play when you get to the highest stage.

You can't rely on one narrow talent or skill for the long haul. Even the adept have to adapt.

In my second year, maybe a week before the season started, my phone rang right after practice. All through training camp I had been struggling. I wasn't shooting as efficiently as I wanted to. My overall numbers were down across the board.

I picked up the call. It was Monta.

We didn't have the strongest relationship my rookie year but I liked him a lot—he was really quiet but capable of sneaking in a memorable one-liner. One time we were all on the court for a shootaround and Monta was a little slow to get going. Some assistant coach, I forget which, yelled out, "Hey Monta, you gonna run this play?"

Monta sniffed the air, a quick snort.

"I don't smell no popcorn popping, do ya?" he said. "You want it now or you want it later?"

I still use that line.

But from a basketball perspective, we really didn't connect on the X's and O's, and as teammates we had never built a strong sense of trust.

So his call felt a little out of the blue.

"Yo, just let me know, are you feeling pressure?" he asked.

"Yeah," I said.

"You're dealing with expectations. I'm dealing with the same stuff."

He said he could see that I was overthinking on the court, which I was. He opened up about similar feelings he'd had as a younger player and how easy it could be to let critics set up shop in your mind, peppering you with opinions while you're trying your best to do what you love.

He told me, "Just play basketball the way you know how."

Monta didn't have to do that for me. Nobody has to do that. I'm sure he was partly motivated by the knowledge that the team needed me to play well for us to have any chance to win that year. We were running it back with me and him in the backcourt. But he had seen how the team had changed from when he was the young guy on the squad in the "We Believe" era. Now all those guys were gone and he was the veteran—even though he was just about to turn 25, he was starting his sixth year in the league.

He was young but stepping into that role. I had to recognize his evolution, too. The tone of our relationship was changing. And that short conversation helped get me out of that funk.

The body responds to the mind.
An obstacle to the work can help you see how much you love the work.

Let that clarity and gratitude drive you.

I'd never played with injuries. I rolled my left ankle one college game in my junior year—playing against Furman on Valentine's Day, with 10 minutes remaining in the second half—but I remembered that game more because my girlfriend Ayesha had come to South Carolina and was sitting in the stands with two signs, HURRY CURRY and BE MY VALENTINE. At 21, we were in the stage of dating when I cooked frozen Red Baron pizzas for us and on special nights we went to the nearby Outback. We still know each other's orders: Caesar salad and steak for me, coconut shrimp for her.

That Valentine's Day, Ayesha had come down to see me play for the first time. Her presence made it one of my favorite wins of the season, even with the sprain. But the injury was mercifully minor; I missed one game and was back the following Saturday.

But now in my second year in the league, just a year and a half after the Valentine's Day sprain, I kept rolling and spraining my right ankle. The incident I remember most clearly was on December 8, 2010. We were playing the San Antonio Spurs and I was having one of my rare runs on the floor. I got an outlet pass, turned to run, and just rolled my ankle. On my own. I didn't touch nobody.

I've seen players land on someone's foot at an unlucky angle and turn their ankles, but nobody was near me. That's when I realized that I might have a real problem. In my first season, the question I had to answer for myself was, *Am I good enough to thrive in this league?* But now the question was, **Am I healthy enough to play at all?**

This was a new challenge: enduring the mental exhaustion of the cycle of injury and surgery and rehab and re-injury. And it went on for 18 months.

I'm grateful for that trial now—and for the gift of experiencing it when I was young and naïve. It became a period of unusual focus: All I was trying to do was get healthy. Get my two feet on the floor so I'd have a chance to be the player I wanted to be.

I had my first ankle surgery in May of 2011. The NBA lockout started on July 1, a result of the breakdown of two years of negotiations between the players' union and the team owners, who demanded cuts to the values of existing and future contracts, plus a hard salary cap. When the union wouldn't settle, owners called a lockout, barring players from setting foot in our team facilities or doing any training with staff. We didn't know that training camps wouldn't be open until December. Ayesha and I got married that July 30 in the same Charlotte church where we'd met nine years earlier. We bought a house in Charlotte to be close to family as we made plans to start our own.

I didn't know how to use my free time while recovering from surgery. My life had been centered around travel, games, and most of all, practice: pre-practice routine, practice, post-practice recovery.

Amidst all this change, **I had a hard time finding my bearings.** But my patience was about to pay off.

The first time Klay Thompson came into the Warriors' locker room, he sat down, kicked his feet up in his locker, pulled out a newspaper, and started reading. It was December and we were about to begin the 2011–2012 season after the resolution of the lockout. Klay had been drafted in the first round, the eleventh overall pick, and like me, he'd grown up with a dad in the NBA. Unlike me, here it was an hour and a half before his first game, and he looked totally comfortable. At peace.

After the team's tumultuous last two seasons, this felt like a new beginning. Klay, and our new coach, Mark Jackson, were part of a culture change across the organization. Now everybody was welcome to bring their whole selves into the locker room. Every personality could just *be*.

The pieces on the team—players, coaches, culture—started to fit a little bit better. But more important, even when things didn't totally click, I felt **we were all on the same journey to figure it out.**

We had no real idea of what we were about to embark on.

There were two team buses heading to Sacramento for a game on March 13, 2012, and I was on the first. Our bus arrived at the arena and the rest of the players headed to the visitors' locker room to get taped up and prepped for the game. I went with them but wasn't getting dressed because of my right ankle. Again. Two days earlier I'd managed to play 10 minutes in a game against the Clippers before I felt that familiar twinge of pain.

The mood was a little quiet and ominous in the locker room. It wasn't because we were playing bad—we thought we still had enough time to make a run for the playoffs—but because it was 48 hours before the trade deadline. That last window always makes players jumpy, but today seemed worse than usual. *What's going on?* I thought.

I looked up at a TV playing in the locker room. At the bottom of the screen there was a banner—"Breaking News: Warriors trade Monta Ellis, Ekpe Udoh, and Kwame Brown for Andrew Bogut."

Just then, Monta showed up in the locker room from the second bus, just off the phone with his agent. He handled the news well, understandably hurt but resolute. We said our goodbyes through shock, and the three traded players left.

Just after that, Coach Jackson pulled me out of the locker room. He was my height, maybe a little shorter, but he always compensated for the height difference between himself and his players by putting a hand on our shoulders to draw us in.

"Yo, I just had to let you know," he said, quiet so only I could hear. "They wanted you in the trade."

They? Which they? Milwaukee or Golden State? Coach Jackson bulldozed ahead. "For whatever reason, it didn't go down like that."

He paused, gripped my shoulder harder. "I kinda stepped in," said Coach Jackson. "I told them **I'm gonna give you the keys.** I really believe in you. We just gotta get you healthy."

I nodded. "Right."

"That's what the rest of the season is gonna be about, getting healthy. But then you're getting the keys to the team."

I nodded again.

"I said we can be a championship-caliber team with you running the show." He dropped his voice even lower. "Don't make me a liar."

"You're getting the keys to the team."

I was not ready for that message.

You may not be ready for the invitation to level up when it comes, but there's this phrase my friend and security guard Yusef Wright gave me that I have grown to like: **When the student is ready, the teacher will appear.** The teacher won't necessarily change who you are or your approach to what you're doing, but they help you have a new perception of yourself. Or they simply tell you, *It's time*.

They can lay the vision out for you, but you have to step into it. In that moment, with Coach Jackson, the vision was that I could be more than a great basketball player. I could be a leader.

It wasn't just that I wasn't ready for that message that I was going to lead the team. *The idea scared the hell out of me.* I had confidence, but I've also always had a healthy insecurity. Just like faith is not the complete absence of doubt, and courage is not the absence of fear, confidence doesn't mean you are free from insecurity. **Earned confidence gives you the capacity to believe the vision but retain the healthy insecurity to ask some questions.** It's the voice that sees what could be and says, "Alright, cool. But how are we gonna do this?"

Coach Jackson was an incredible motivator with a gift for making us believe him. In the locker room before a game, he was a pastor-storyteller, inspiring us one day to be our best selves, and the next, filling us with made-up grievances against the other team. We were a team trying to find our identity and a belief to build it on. The identity he proposed for us was: "We can beat any team, any given night." Not "will," but "can." We really did have the talent to win—and if some of us were still a little unsure, Coach breathed the confidence into us to go out and play like we did.

With my injuries still nagging me that third season—I only played 26 games—and realizing I was headed for another surgery in the off-season, I needed that kind of belief. We ended the shortened lockout season with a 23-43 record, missing the playoffs. But we were starting to get shot ready—into position so that **when the ball bounced our way, we had the confidence we needed to be a serious threat.**

When I went under the knife the second time in April of 2012, doctors told me there were three potential scenarios. If I was lucky, they would only need to do a clean-up of my right ankle, which would also offer a quick recovery period—three to four months. Or they might discover that I needed a full reconstruction, which would require an estimated six-month recovery period, but with uncertain results. Or perhaps some deeper intervention was needed, with an uncertain timetable for walking, let alone playing in the NBA. When I went under, there was a lot I couldn't know.

But I always know my faith. That faith is the centering force in my life. Every position God has put me in—whether it's an NBA court or an operating room—he has placed me there to help others. I leaned again on Romans 8:28, the words that fortify me through every season of life.

The surgical team sent a camera into my ankle first, which revealed to them a junkyard of past injuries, a crud of tissue flecked with cartilage—but no structural damage. With great relief, I listened as they explained they were able to clean out the scar tissue and loose debris. I would be able to get back to the court.

That time was so scary, but also a blessing. **The gift of fear is that you realize what you're grateful for**—in my case, the ability to do the work I love with the support system I had.

Rehab is the hardest thing I have ever done in my life. People now know how the story ends, but at the time I could not see the light at the end of the tunnel. I went to the rehab facility every day, literally just putting one foot in front of the other. I felt completely cut off from the team. I realized in that moment that **for all my ambition to be the best player in the world, more than that, I just wanted to play the game I loved.**

The two surgeries were vital, but what I did *after* the surgeries is what made the real difference in my career. During my recovery, I reached out to as many people as I could to ask them about how to take care of my body a little bit better. With the help of Keke Lyles, who would become the Warriors' director of performance, **I learned what it really means to get stronger**—not just bulking up, but retraining my movement patterns to be more efficient and strengthening my core. Lyles introduced me to alternative bodywork I'd never done before, like hyper-specific yoga poses for my hips and trap-bar deadlifts for the glutes. I practically got a degree in human anatomy, learning how every piece of your body's puzzle fits together. I was open to all of these new ways of becoming a better, stronger, healthier player, but I was only in that space because the injuries put me there.

If that's all I'd be able to do,
then that's what I'd do.
But I had to do it.

Life has an interesting way of revealing what you need to do by putting you in the place you need to be. I didn't realize it at the time, but even through my injuries I was learning to lead—not through my voice, which I hadn't really found yet, but by example. Every day I kept showing up to get better. That consistency—visible to my teammates, but also to the coaches, the fans, and even the media—created a sense of trust, which is the bedrock of leadership.

I was—through the losses and doubts, the times on the bench or in rehab—where I needed to be.

Life has put you somewhere you need to be. It's up to you to be ready to take your shot.

Part 2

Leader

The Height of the Arc

Your objective as a player is to make the game as easy as possible.

I started covering more ground and shooting threes from longer distances to solve a problem. Sometimes the biggest revolutions—in sports, in business, in technology, in politics—start with two simple questions: Why is this so hard? How can I make it easier?

My problem as an offensive player was the defense, and the solution was space. The farther out I went, the more space I created between myself and the defenders. The more space I had, the easier the game became.

That was my thought process. I was just reacting to how I was being guarded. It's true in basketball and in other parts of life, too. The farther you get from your competition, the harder it is for them to defend your shot. So let's get to shooting.

There was an audacity to shooting so much from so far out, it's true. But when they started to go in, I established for myself that it wasn't luck. **I couldn't help but think, Let's get another one.**

At the time, no one was using the deep three as a weapon the way I thought I could. I sank an NBA-record 272 three-pointers in the 2012–2013 season, 106 more than the NBA leader in three-pointers the season before. The average distance of those three-pointers was about a foot farther from the basket than the rest of the league's threes— and that number would grow from year to year.

Discernment—the judgment it takes to make smart, disciplined decisions—can be taught.

My coach in college, Bob McKillop, gave everyone on the team a different "license to shoot." Everybody knew which spots on the floor they were allowed to shoot from because Coach had made it clear in a one-on-one conversation. Coach would say to two other players who he knew would try it that they could *not* shoot a three above the arc. "If you shoot one from the corner, that's fine, but if you shoot one from over there, I will take you out." My license was that I could shoot from anywhere, but the point is, I had to earn it and it could've been revoked.

College is when a coach can micromanage you a little bit more, but the kind of discipline he imposed on our shot selection helped me internalize what a good shot is. By the time I got to the NBA and the Warriors, Coach Jackson accepted my unusual shot selection without us ever having to have a formal talk about it. I didn't have anybody checking me, because I didn't need anyone to check me. Coach Jackson trusted me because he knew I was taking shots I had practiced a thousand times—and when I started hitting them, he didn't want to pour water on the fire.

When I'm shooting logo shots, the mechanics are the exact same as all those shots I've taken in the paint. If you're not perfect shooting right in front of the basket, there's no way you're going to be perfect behind that three-point line.

You add range to your mechanics. It doesn't work the other way around.

As my three-point volume and efficiency increased, other players changed their games to try to match it, and not just in the NBA. Nine-year-olds started jacking 40-footers as soon as they walked in the gym. And missing while they're yelling out "Curry!" (By the way, stop tagging me in all those horrible clips of people taking bad shots. I did not tell that person to take that shot.) Some people call them the Curry Generation, but I don't like the term; when I meet them at my camps, I reel them in from the start: **"There's a process. It ends in joy. But it starts in the paint."**

You don't just one day wake up and become a leader any more than a team can show up to the gym one day and play like champions. You grow into it.

As I started my fourth season with Golden State, the whole team was on a crazy learning curve: We were playing meaningful basketball games for the first time and learning about each other on the fly.

We were hungry. Our record still put us in the middle of the pack, but there were moments when I'd hear a commentator say we could win a championship—and it wasn't as a punchline to a joke. None of us on that team had ever won *anything,* so even thinking about a chip put us in new emotional territory. I could see a new opportunity in front of us and a coach behind us with an amazing ability to infuse belief into our locker room.

As you evo[lve]
to teammates
doing t[h]

ve, be open
and partners
e same.

Klay and I made the most out of competing with each other in practice—we both just loved shooting the ball and were happy for the chance to do it. He'd spent his rookie year fighting to get minutes on the court as I was dealing with injuries.

If I was teaching somebody basketball from scratch, like molding them from clay—no pun intended—I would teach them Klay Thompson's form with the admonishment that "This is how you *should* shoot." Because **Klay's shot is structurally, well, perfect.** Everything is stacked, his release point's high and a little off to the side so he can see the rim.

As perfect as his form is, if I try to shoot like Klay, I'll miss. His style is too rigid for the way my body is put together. I have a loosey-goosey vibe, down to my pointing my feet just a little farther left of the target than normal. And visually, it's not as pretty as Klay's.

Klay's form is interesting because his personality is so far from rigid. Playing with him was a constant reminder that the game is supposed to be fun.

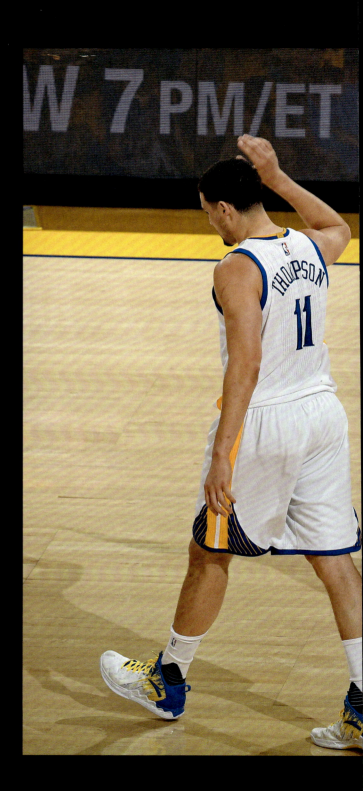

One of the rookies just the other day asked me, real quiet, "Yo, what's your take on trash-talking?"

I thought for a second. "It's not necessary for me to use it as a competitive element," I answered. "But I like good material."

On the court, if you say something to me, I'm going to say something back. But a funny facial expression or a smile that shows I'm enjoying myself out there—that's actually a more powerful comeback than huffing and puffing. Then I throw in a shimmy 'cause they *hate* that.

Be ready for someone to disrespect you on the court. Take it in and turn it on its head—make it a compliment. **No one tries to diminish you unless they see you as a threat.**

I love turning things on their head and making them useful. I once heard about a monk who reminds himself to breathe and meditate whenever he hears a siren. The guy disrespecting you is the siren. Breathe, and know you have the upper hand.

What's the recipe for a championship roster?

Put away the stat sheets. When you're putting together a championship team, you need teammates whose contributions aren't counted in stats. I'm talking about someone who the box score will tell you played fifteen minutes and produced five rebounds, two points, maybe an assist—but if you watch the game, you see his presence everywhere. The energy, the playmaking, the basketball IQ—those are the elements that make a player essential to a winning team.

A casual fan might not see it if someone doesn't point it out, but other players see it clearly. If you're a team leader, you want *that* guy on the team and hate to see him playing against you.

When you are looking for someone to partner with in a business venture, you have to be careful about selecting someone who's just like you—**you don't get much from redundant, overlapping skills and approaches.** The same applies when you're trying to build a winning team culture in basketball. If there were two Steph Currys leading our team—two players who were reserved and stoic in their approach to leadership—our locker room would be missing the energy (and even just the literal volume) that's needed to inspire a team to greatness. You need steady, resolute, quiet leadership sometimes and sometimes you need someone who'll just stir things up. Luckily, we found just the right man for the job.

Of course, I am talking about Draymond Green. He was the steal of the 2012 NBA Draft, the 35th overall draft pick, and he transformed our team. You won't necessarily perceive his gifts just looking at what's on the stat sheet, but he's going to pass the eye test every single time. He simply makes winning plays. Every time.

People talk about the "telepathy" Draymond and I share, our ability to know two steps ahead of time what the other will do. We had to build that level of connection over time, but honestly, almost right away we had pretty good chemistry in terms of knowing how to work together off the ball. Then year by year we built on that chemistry with trust—which allowed us to go deeper and start experimenting. Gradually we started to understand that our team worked best with me and Klay off the ball and with Draymond handling it. It was unusual to have a forward like Dray in that role, but his drive and intelligence and our growing chemistry opened up all kinds of creative possibilities for our offense. It was unconventional but we knew that if we got the ball to Draymond, he would make the right play.

Now we had three key pieces: me, Klay, and Draymond. Still young, still trying to figure out what was possible. Did we know we were building up to a dynasty? Uh, no. We *never* would have called it that while we were fighting our way into the middle of the standings.

But there was this one game.

It was in Miami—on 12/12/12—during the era of the Big Three down there: Bron, D.Wade, and Chris Bosh. The Heat were the NBA champions.

The game was tied with about 12 seconds left when we called a timeout. Coach Jackson didn't draw up a play for any specific player to take the last shot—the plan was to see who was open and make the best play. On another team, the go-to might have been me or Klay, even if we had to force it. But the Warriors were different. Jarrett Jack dribbled the ball at the top of the key during the final possession and was about to shoot when he found Draymond wide open under the basket. Draymond hit the winning layup with less than a second left.

We watched that clip together this year—it was kind of funny because more than the game, we were watching all of our reactions on the court that day right after Dray hit the layup. We celebrated like we'd just won Game 7 of the Finals.

That game changed us. We'd won games before, of course, but this was a win against the best team in the league, the defending champs. Now we were showing people what we were capable of—like Coach Jackson promised, in any given game we could beat any team. And **we were going to bring it every night.**

Another special night was just around the corner.

February 27, 2013, against the Knicks at the Garden.

I knew the game was special during the middle of the second quarter. I already had scored the last 15 in a row when I pulled up for a three in transition. It was a heat-check shot, a wilder, more difficult shot than you'd normally take, but when things are really flowing, when you feel like just about anything is going to go in, you want to test just how locked in you are. The shot went in.

We lost the game, unfortunately, but Coach Jackson played me all 48 minutes and I scored 54 points, a career high at the time. I was just happy I had my legs. Until then, the narrative about me always returned to my injury history and my size.

It was Doris Burke, the first woman to announce for the Knicks on TV or radio, who said it: "For a guy who a lot of people questioned, at six-three and 185 pounds, could he be effective in the league? He has put those concerns to rest."

That game changed the narrative. People had to take me seriously. It was no longer a question. I'd proven that I had game.

I was asked afterward what was going on in my mind as I was playing and that's when I realized that on the best scoring night of my career to that point, there had been no internal dialogue: This was the most unconscious I had ever been shooting the basketball. The action swirled all around me but inside I was still.

But after the game the noise came flooding back in. I thought about the list of guys who'd scored 50-plus at Madison Square Garden: Jordan, LeBron, Kobe, Bernard King on Christmas '84 . . . and that snapped me out of the stillness. The game was over. I could now fully feel how special a night this was.

We finally made the playoffs in 2013—the Warriors' first time making it since 2007. We were going in as a number-6 seed with a record of 47-35. Our first-round opponent was the Denver Nuggets, the third seed. We lost the first game but won the second. It was after that one that Coach Jackson gave the press a phrase that would spark a thousand think pieces and rebuttals: "Klay Thompson and Steph Curry, in my opinion, they're the greatest shooting backcourt in the history of the game."

Reporters gave him a million "what abouts" to qualify it, but he held tight and added, "Call my bluff."

Somewhere inside of me I may have allowed myself the thought that Klay and I were doing something special, but hearing someone take that megaphone to say he believed in you, when everyone's laughing? Neither Klay nor I would have ever said it ourselves, but when Coach Jackson put his own reputation on the line and said it, it empowered us to quietly say to ourselves, *Well, maybe we are*.

"Call my bluff," Coach said. **When someone vouches for you like that, the pressure to prove them right is a powerful motivator,** stronger even than the need to prove someone else wrong. We were determined to back him up.

When I take a long shot and have full, 100 percent confidence that the ball is going into the basket, I sometimes turn and run back down the court while the ball is still in the air. This has been called "the no-look three," and the first time I ever did it was in Game 4 of that first playoff series against Denver in 2013. We were at Oracle. I'd gone on a crazy run midway through the third quarter, knocking them down left and right—22 points in six and a half minutes.

One of the last ones that quarter was an open three in the corner, right in front of Denver's bench. You can imagine the trash talk behind me. Well, maybe you can't. But it was bad.

But that just gave me an extra boost of motivation as I rose up for the shot. When I let go, and the ball left my finger, I thought, *I have never felt a shot like that.*

It was going in. There was no doubt in my mind.

I turned back downcourt before the ball even hit the height of the arc. I didn't need to watch it. As I turned, I stared down the players on the Denver bench. And then I kept moving, heading back on defense as the shot finally swished through the net.

Someone asked me once, "But how do you know if the shot goes in?"
The answer is obvious to me. "The crowd," I said.
I've missed on no-look threes. That's going to happen with you, too. You're going to be so confident that you've nailed something—on the court or in life—that you've already moved on to the next thing by the time you find out you missed.

There is good news, though. You're already in motion. **And the next one is going in.**

One of the things I like about the no-look three is that me turning my back on the actual result has always been received for what it is: a sign of decisive faith, not a lack of caring. Believe me, I'm waiting to hear that crowd.

You cannot be great and act with doubt. Whatever your endeavor, keep your mind full of positive thoughts about that goal being met. **Trust in your preparation and believe in your ability**—the things you can control—and your confidence will give you a huge advantage.

A team has to work to deserve its fans. Back then, I didn't know nothing about Oracle or the Dub Nation fan base.

Then we got to the playoffs. Twenty minutes before each home game—when the fans are still filing in and the arena is only 75 percent full— the crowd would already be chanting *Warriors*.

With all due respect to other fan bases, Warriors fans are geniuses in the art of cheering. There's nothing like it.

It starts with their understanding of the flow of the game. They set the tone early—before the game even starts— so the other team feels the home-court energy as soon as they walk into the place. As a player, you don't want your home crowd to be waiting silently for something to happen before they erupt. Dub Nation is intentional about creating that energy right away.

And then they come through with oceanic waves of cheering in the big moments and after the great shots—but there's something deeper about the relationship between this crowd and the team. There are times when you've missed three possessions in a row. You're feeling a little demoralized and frustrated. A whistle. Maybe a timeout. There's a dead ball. And the fans get it. You can feel them collectively thinking, *Alright, we need some life. It don't have to be like this*.

They get up and they let you know they're here. It's not just a loud arena responding to good plays. It's a home crowd supporting its team, giving us life when we need it. I wish that for every player, but you can't have Dub Nation. They're the ultimate home-court advantage.

That first playoff series was the first time I felt every single one of those fans pushing the team higher.

We beat the Nuggets in six, then moved on to face the Spurs. They were the champs, and we got beat. We lost a 17-point lead in the fourth quarter of Game 2. We got it back to a one-point lead at 127–126 with about three seconds left. That's when Manu Ginobili hit a game-winner on us. An absolute dagger.

Losing, for me, is the worst feeling in life. I get over it, I learn from it, I move on—but in the moment, it pushes me into a dark place. It didn't help that people still didn't give us credit for the breakthrough we knew we'd made that season. To label a Warriors team as a title contender was foreign to a lot of NBA gurus.

But the series showed what we could do. When I shook off the immediate devastation of the loss, it was totally clear to me: **We would build on this.** And we'd be back.

Leaders deflect as much credit as possible to the team. Nothing you do great in this world is done by yourself. Your teammates are equity partners—all have to buy in, so we all get to share the profits.

I spent my July 30, 2013, second wedding anniversary in Nyarugusu Refugee Camp in Tanzania. I was there in eastern Africa with Nothing But Nets, a UN Foundation initiative to stop malaria, a leading killer of children in sub-Saharan Africa, spread primarily through mosquitos. Bednets are proven to cut malaria risk by 90 percent, so during the 2012–2013 season, I led the Three for Three challenge, donating three lifesaving bednets for every time I knocked down a three.

That was the year I made the new single-season three-point record with 272 makes. Success can be its own motivation, but **all of my most meaningful achievements come when I play for something bigger than myself.**

I was thousands of miles away from Ayesha and tried to use some kind of satellite phone to tell her what I was seeing. On paper, the fact sheet said there were 60,000 displaced Congolese refugees. As a new parent—our first daughter Riley had just had her first birthday— all I could tell her about was the moms and dads I saw who were unable to protect their kids from malaria. Almost every parent I talked to said their kids had some experience with malaria or had been lost before the age of two, when malaria is most deadly.

I walked through the maternity ward, seeing the moms nursing babies with malaria—those innocent infants, all so wide-eyed and helpless in their mothers' arms but already stricken with this disease. My eye went to a poster on the wall, a current stat sheet of what illnesses the doctors were dealing with, and a morbidity report of the number of children who already died at the camp the previous six months. That number formed a target in my mind—I knew that we could get it down.

Outside, there were some kids who knew about basketball and one had drawn white lines in the red dirt to create a court next to a hoop someone had brought in. It was like middle school in Toronto, or the Y in Charlotte, or those first days of training camp with the Warriors—I once again found myself discovering community and connection among strangers by playing basketball. I offered some coaching and demonstrated some three-pointers, but the big moment—or what I thought would be one—was when I actually dunked the ball. At Oracle this would have been huge—I think I may have dunked three times all of our last season. Maybe. But here, nobody clapped.

"They don't know how hard that was for me," I joked.

The civil rights leader Bryan Stevenson says that to change anything you have to get close to it—but if you get close, you can change the world. I knew this from my time playing basketball: A stat sheet could never tell you more than you learn from getting close to a teammate, watching how they move, how they think, how they respond to pressure, what brings them joy. And I knew from my time at the camp that all the stats in the world would not tell me what I needed to know about what malaria does to individual humans—babies, moms, and dads. Just like I learned from my parents, sports is a language that can transcend differences. So even in that camp, I was able to connect to the people around me and carry their unique individual stories home.

I was motivated, more than ever, to do what I could. I was still just a third-year basketball player, but I left Tanzania with a stronger sense of how I could make my life and leadership matter.

Andre Iguodala came to us from Denver in 2013. Before he came, I'd heard that during the 2011 lockout he spent time shadowing a venture capitalist, which gave me a hint about the kind of teammate we were getting. Andre could keep it light when he needed to, but pretty soon the mix of conversations in the locker room included Dre critiquing a promising tech start-up or analyzing a big brand's profit-and-loss statement in the *Wall Street Journal*.

It was Dre who first made us understand what it meant that we played right in the backyard of Silicon Valley. These major VCs, tech CEOs, and brilliant entrepreneurs and computer scientists were sitting courtside watching *us*. We were in a rare position for professional athletes—we didn't just have to wait for a handful of endorsement deals; we could network with our fans and learn about opportunities in the venture space. I found myself attracted to tech that made people's lives better and companies committed to real equity and access—and who shared an end goal of inspiring people and enhancing opportunities for the next generation.

We met secretly at Oracle after the game. In the extra locker rooms that were always empty, just down the hallway between the home and visiting lockers. It was me and Draymond from our team and Chris Paul, Blake Griffin, and DeAndre Jordan from the Clippers. This was after Game 4 of the 2014 playoffs, the day after Donald Sterling, owner of their team, had been exposed as a racist when a secret recording of him was revealed.

We'd all been texting that weekend and agreed to meet in the bowels of Oracle to plan a response. The Clippers had done a silent protest before Game 4, wearing their warmups inside out. We wanted to support them as we waited for updates from the league's investigation into Sterling. The NBA was led now by Adam Silver, in the job just two months after his predecessor, David Stern, had retired after 30 years. The conversation in that locker room was that if Adam doled out a punishment to Sterling that didn't rise to the level of the crime, we had to act decisively.

"What if we just walked off the court that night?" someone said. "What if when the jump ball is in the air we all just shook hands and walked off the court?"

The statement hung there for a moment while we all pondered the gravity of the situation. The Clippers had been thrust into the situation in the middle of a playoff series when there was already so much pressure on them. It was especially tough on Chris Paul—he was not only a leader on his team, he was also the president of the players' union. But he was a teammate first and joined the team's other leaders to take responsibility for how they were going to respond because that's who they were: professionals with a sense of pride about getting it right and holding power to account. All this while they were trying to prepare to beat us in a playoff series.

Likewise, we wanted to be partners to the Clippers in dealing with the Sterling situation but ruthless competitors when we got on the court.

The morning of Game 5 in L.A., our talks continued in the shootaround. We all had our phones out, waiting for the league's press conference. Finally, Adam Silver took to the podium and announced a lifetime ban against Sterling. He would never be involved with the NBA again, not even allowed to attend a game. It was the result we wanted, and as Warriors, we would respect the Clippers' decision on how they moved forward as a team. The Clippers were not sure what they would come back to when they returned from Golden State. They felt they owed it to those fans to play, so we all just got "back to basketball and doing what we love," as CP said.

And yet . . .

I look back at that moment sometimes and wish we'd done the walkout anyway. Chris and I still talk about it. We all do. We don't know what would have come out of it, but walking out would have leveraged that moment to shift how we were seen as athletes. It would have made a clear statement: We would not tolerate racial injustice for the sake of the NBA's bottom line. Or our own.

But ultimately, I'm not sure. Would it have made a difference? Or would it just punish the players and fans? Would we be the ones suffering because we didn't get to play—or watch—the game we love?

That situation had a ripple effect on how players advocated for themselves and causes in subsequent years, but I remember those secret meetings as a moment that spoke to the special bond between players and the depth of our shared love and respect for the game. We were entrenched rivals—look at the fight the two teams got into over the Clippers celebrating our Game 7 loss—but we were also leaders and caretakers of the game, communicating openly and cooperatively on how to handle the situation.

From the perspective of the players in 2014, Coach Mark Jackson had done a phenomenal job of transforming the culture of the team and empowering us to go to the next level. But there was dysfunction between Coach and upstairs. The Warriors fired him in May, a few days after the playoffs.

Bob Myers had just come in as general manager, and he came to my house to tell me about Jackson's firing personally. He loves telling the story because he says it was the most scared he'd ever be as a GM.

We stood there talking by my garage, which opened out to my home court. I was hot.

But I listened. He laid out his reasons, and I was straight with him. "I don't like this decision because I love Coach," I said. But I had to think big-picture as a team leader.

"I understand why you're doing this," I said, "but if you're going to fire him, you better get it right." I left it there, but he knew what I meant: **The next coach had to be exceptional.**

Steve Kerr was a five-time championship player—three alongside Michael Jordan on the Bulls and two with San Antonio—whose retirement plan began as a commentator before he became general manager of the Phoenix Suns. He was supposedly about to take his first coaching job ever with the New York Knicks, but the deal wasn't set yet. Once the Warriors job opened up he took a meeting. And he realized what we could all do together.

When a new coach comes in, it's awkward at first. As a player—and a leader of the team—I was proud of the work we'd done to become championship contenders. So who is this guy coming in wanting to be the hero who makes us great?

But **Coach Kerr approached us with real humility** from the first meeting. "I don't want to come in here and re-create the wheel," he said, "but with a couple tweaks in how we approach our offensive playbook, we can win a championship based on what we already have."

As a coach, he knew the value he was bringing, but he acknowledged that the team was already made to win. We needed to hear that then.

It disarmed me, which in hindsight is a great tactic for a leader. *Okay,* I thought, *I can roll with this.*

The March 8, 2015, game against the Clippers comes up again and again when people talk about my relationship with Coach Kerr.

One of my good friends, Ekpe Udoh, was playing for the Clippers that year. Before the game, we got a chance to catch up during warmups. I was on a little heater leading up to that game, so right before the game begins, Ekpe yelled out to me, "Yo, don't be doing no crazy stuff."

It was a challenge.

Nine minutes left in the third quarter. I looked over at Ekpe sitting on the bench. Andrew Bogut tossed me the ball and I drove toward the paint. I did a little crossover to stay away from Matt Barnes, who was defending me, and then dribbled through my legs and behind my back, moving back toward the arc, to get some distance from Spencer Hawes and DeAndre Jordan, who were closing the paint. Chris Paul pressed in on me, bumping my thigh, and I thought, *He's gonna steal it*—he has stolen the ball from me plenty of times—but I danced away as he swiped and missed. After all that I was kind of surprised the ball had come back into my hands without being stolen, and my momentum carried me into a shot, a fadeaway three-pointer.

As I was going up, I noticed Draymond out of the corner of my eye, pointing at Klay, who was wide open on the right wing. But it was too late to pass it off, I was already in motion.

As the ball floated through the net, Coach Kerr threw his hands on his head, shocked that I took the shot. And maybe even more shocked that I made it. That's the moment everyone focused on later.

But I wasn't looking at Coach—I was looking at Ekpe. As soon as I'd gone up, he crossed his arms and slumped on the bench like, *Look at this fool*.

That's as close as I got to getting my license taken away by Coach. But it ended up having the opposite effect. For the first time, he acknowledged that he wouldn't tell us what a bad shot is. **This was what me and Klay needed—trust.** Once we had that, we could stretch our shot-taking creativity and imaginations. We could redefine what a good shot was. Now that kind of offensive creativity became part of the team's DNA.

My phone buzzed with a text. I didn't look at it.

I was in a hotel room after Game 3 of the 2015 playoffs. We'd run up against the Grizzlies. We won the first one, then got beat bad twice. Once at home, and now in Memphis.

Another text. I didn't look. I had a tendency back then, after a tough loss, to go straight to watching the film and looking inward to try to figure out what's going on. *Then* I'd give some direction or leadership on what we all need to do. I was afraid to let my emotions go first and then have to reel it back in after review and reflection.

"I have to play better for us to win games, especially on the road," I said in the press conference right after. "I hold myself to a high standard. I haven't reached it yet." Coach Kerr said it was part of the process. "You see teams go through this all the time in the playoffs," he said. "It's the only way to figure it out, to go through the pain of losing a game like tonight."

We'd made a clear leap as a team that season and even people who doubted us before said we'd had a chance to win it all. Forget the forecasters, *we* felt it. We'd finished the regular season with a league-best record of 67–15 and I got my first MVP. None of that means anything once the playoffs start. You want to win it all so bad—you fight tooth and nail all season to get into a position to get it, and you feel like you are right there at the breakthrough moment . . .

. . . and suddenly you're in Memphis scrambling to close a 19-point lead. Shooting ten outside the arc and making two. One loss, you can say they snuck a win in. But two?

I'd watched the game once already, reliving every possession. And now I was playing Mario Tennis on the Nintendo 64. Just by myself, in isolation, trying to distract myself from the possibility of a devastating series loss, and someone's blowing me up.

It was Draymond. "Yo, let's go to Blues City Café," he texted. "Meet me there. No excuses."

Excuses? I thought. The barbecue joint was across Beale Street. "Alright," I typed. "10 minutes."

I put my hood up to walk over. Memphis is a small town, but it's buzzing. You can get lost in the crowd on Beale Street.

A red neon sign, KITCHEN OPEN LATE, greeted me at the door, and I walked into a too-bright, packed room of metal chairs at Formica tables. Draymond was in the back room posted up waiting for me with Festus Ezeli and David Lee. He'd already ordered me a beer. "Everybody's panicked," he said. I nodded, taking my spot in the old-fashioned booth with high backs so you can really talk. People kept a respectful distance from the dead men walking.

The four of us talked about the game for a second—going over the things that would have changed the outcome for us. I don't even drink during the playoffs and I had about three beers. And eventually we all kind of let go of the angst and the pressures we were putting on ourselves, which were heavier than ever because we were so close to kind of breaking through. "Hey, we're in the playoffs," we said. "We know we're still a good team. Let's come back and take care of business."

In getting me out of the room, and out of my head, Draymond was doing what he always does: Looking for a way to get me open. To give me a shot.

Then I could take that energy and lead in my way, by getting out of my own way. Decompress a little bit so that I had the mental space the next day at film and at practice to say what I needed to say knowing that everybody is going to feed off of *that* energy.

Because I know this: If I come into practice like a zombie—in my head and not saying anything—they're gonna think that I'm doubting *myself,* which then makes the team doubt *itself*.

That loss led to a win Monday. And then to the next two wins, which advanced us to the Conference Finals against Houston. We beat them in five games, advancing us to the Finals against the Cleveland Cavaliers. We always look back at that night, when we felt like the world was ending, as the start of our run at greatness.

As a leader, your instinct might be to avoid emotion and not think as a teammate. Off the court, in my family and as a business partner, my instincts are to be a fixer. I've always got an answer, but it can come at the cost of meeting the emotion in the moment. **Sometimes leading by example is allowing yourself to be human, too.**

When I talk about that championship season and the Finals in 2015, I understand why people focus on Game 6, when we won the whole thing in Cleveland. Of course, it was a huge moment for the Warriors. But Game 5, home at Oracle, is the one that taught us that you don't know what it takes to get over the hump until you do it.

Leading up to that game, I had—to my standards—a couple of rough games, particularly Game 2 and Game 3 after our win in Game 1. This was a pivotal swing game with the series tied 2–2. We were at home. So we needed this one before we had to go back to Cleveland.

Before the game, I told the team not to be discouraged if LeBron James made shots. He was going to. "Stick with the program," I said. Sometimes when you're *in* the moment, things move fast. You can feel the moment slipping out of your hands. Choose not to. **Let them try to take it from you, but don't let it slip away.**

I couldn't anticipate the new level of freedom that winning a championship would give the team. When you get one, you get greedy. Because the stress of getting that first one, 82 games locked in, then more games in the playoffs—you've got to keep your head down. But when you win, you get to look up again. You get to feel the euphoria of final victory.

And when it's over, you have something you never had before: It is no longer a mystery how hard it is to win a championship. You realize you had to be that locked in all season long. You could not afford to let go of a regular season game in December. And you never will again.

That knowledge is a responsibility. You now have to breathe that into the people who've joined your team because of your success. You can't just give the rookies your confidence, you must show them that **every game—every possession, every shot—matters.**

With any championship team, people are going to talk about what had to go right for you to win. They don't want to acknowledge that success is a choice. Yes, there's luck, but first and foremost, **you have to put yourself in a position where the ball is gonna bounce your way.**

We were about to have a near-perfect 2015–2016 season, but the work for that began that summer, when the narrative around the league was that we'd just gotten lucky with the championship.

"Cleveland was hurt" was all we heard.

That became our motivation. We were going to use the next season to validate the last one. "Let's just go" was a line I kept saying. "Every single game." We had off-the-charts confidence and our team chemistry was unrivaled. We played together on the court and hung out off the court, all of us **locked into a shared vision.**

Heading into December we were 24-0. That incredible streak made every game like the Finals—the intensity bonded us even more. Then we came to Milwaukee and saw an arena full of fans wearing "24-1" shirts that turned out to be prophetic. They pulled an upset.

But we still had a goal to reach that kept us playing at an extremely high level every single game. That goal was the 1995–1996 Chicago Bulls' record of 72-10, the untouchable standard for 20 years.

"Let's just go," I said.

It was one of those Saturday-night prime-time games. The stakes were high that February 27, 2016: The Oklahoma City Thunder was a super-tough team, competing with us for the top of the West. Our record was 52-5—I know that because I just looked it up—and I was shooting the ball better than I ever had. The game was going to be the culmination of an amazing week. That Tuesday morning after beating Atlanta, me and Andre Iguodala fulfilled a lifelong dream of mine, playing golf at Augusta National, home of the PGA Masters Tournament, for the first time. Then we beat Miami, then Orlando.

The conversation among the team was about the Bulls' record. Was it really in reach? Could we keep the pace up?

If you looked at the start of the game in OKC, the answer was no. We were down 15–8, but I still felt I was shooting extremely well.

And then, just a little over a minute into the second half, Russell Westbrook came down hard on my foot. I rolled my left ankle.

When you get hurt, your emotions go all over the place. In a split second I was pulled back into those early years of agony, injury, recovery, and an enduring narrative that I'd never be healthy enough to be a star. I was feeling the weight of everyone staring at me on the floor like it was over. Again. Anytime it's my ankle, when I feel that familiar sensation of pain, fear threatens to take over. So, lying there on the floor of the arena, the first thing I had to conquer was just the fear of getting up. Trying to put weight on it. When I finally did, I realized I could walk. Gingerly, but I could walk—a world of difference from the old days. This was what I had worked for. Injuries happen, I would tell myself during all those hours of PT and conditioning. But when it inevitably occurred, would I be strong enough to walk away? And here I was.

"Okay," I said. "I need to get retaped." I made it to the locker room, feeling like a dead man walking with everyone looking at me. But I made it. This was different. Could I go back in the game? Even if my body could, I needed to get my mind right.

Retaped, I came back out of the locker room and sat courtside on the floor in front of the scorer's table, no chair, just sitting on my butt, legs sprawled out as I processed what had happened.

I needed to feel the floor beneath me so I could ground myself. I did some deep breathing and had a conversation with the pain. It was smaller now, leaving me. *Okay,* I said silently. *Let's get back into what I was trying to do.*

I scored 31 more points, eventually making 8 of 11 threes. We were down five points with under a minute left when Klay hit a three right in front of their bench. Then we got a steal and Andre was fouled and made two free-throws with 0.7 seconds left in the game. And if anybody knows Andre and his free-throw percentage . . . well, he had to step up and have ice in his veins. And he did.

OKC's Kevin Durant missed a hook shot at the buzzer, so we went into overtime. It was a mid-season game, but the stakes felt high. **Moments like this are what makes sports so glorious.** The whole building could feel it.

The energy in the arena was electric. I made two more threes in overtime. And then, with the score tied again at 118–118, Westbrook missed a shot. We fought for the rebound and I got it. There was no doubt in my mind I was shooting, it was just a matter of where. My only thought was that I wanted to shoot before the defense got set. André Roberson was going to try to stop me and I couldn't let him. What's funny is that Anthony Morrow—who used to be my teammate on the Warriors after I played against him in high school—was on the OKC bench, and as soon as I got to half-court, he started yelling and waving at the defender. Like, Get up! Get a hand higher! He's from Charlotte and he *knew*. A.Mo could see where I was heading. Everybody *but* the guys on the court could see it.

But I knew as long as I got it off, it was going in.

I hit that last shot, with .06 seconds left, a three-pointer from 38 feet. That's when announcer Mike Breen let off his infamous double bang. "Bang! Bang! Oh, what a shot from Curry!"

I'd made game-winners before, but from that deep? Everything, all the work and rehab and bonding and growing into leadership, all of it built up to that. I'd taken that shot in practice, but this was different. **You work on the shot, perfect the shot, but then you still gotta have the audacity to take the shot.** I took it.

I was in my living room in May, about to head to the practice facility. I knew I was going to get my second MVP, but the question was if it would be unanimous or not.

If it was unanimous, it would be the first time in NBA history, but that's not why it mattered to me. It meant that not only was I being acknowledged as a great individual player, but that those voters knew our team was historically great. We were playing amazing basketball as a team, but even if we weren't, you never get MVP in spite of your team—you win the honor because of the people you play with. It would give me a huge sense of pride in what we'd all accomplished.

My back was to the TV, right over my head. The news popped up and my memory of it is the reaction of my friends and family: They went nuts.

It was unanimous.

We'd just had a come-from-behind victory over the Portland Trail Blazers in the 2016 Western Conference Semifinals on the day of the ceremony. Eventually we'd take on the Cleveland Cavaliers in the Finals again.

During the Q&A, I was asked how I wanted to be remembered, which is what happens to you as soon as you're handed a trophy.

"There is a God-given ability and talents and things like that," I said. **"But I want to be remembered as somebody who worked hard."**

You work to be prepared, and nerves are the crucial test of the preparation. Even more than an opponent, you first have to respond to your nerves. How do you respond? **If you're doubting yourself, it's very possible you did not prepare enough.**

And sometimes, because you're human, you will have moments when despite all your preparation, you still feel that thing you want slipping away. And that's when your nerves can overwhelm all of your self-control and practiced calm.

The room starts spiraling. You start trying to do things you're just not equipped to do.

You start playing outside yourself.

Welcome to my nightmare. Welcome to Game 7 of the 2016 Finals.

My ultimate experience of losing control came at the worst possible time: the last minute of Game 7 of the 2016 Finals.

When I get asked to describe a winning streak, I struggle to give words to the feeling. But I can tell you exactly what that last minute felt like. Helplessness. I was trying to connect my body and my mind. I had no idea how to do it in that moment, but I was *trying*. Somehow that makes it worse.

There's always going to be a part of me that can go right back there—one of those nightmares that keep happening.

We're tied 89–89 at Oracle, June 19, 2016. I've just badly missed a three-point attempt on our end. With 1:09 remaining, Cleveland takes a timeout. When play resumes, Kyrie Irving and I are isolated at the arc. Kyrie takes a shot over me. It goes in. The seconds tick off. I miss a shot on our end and eventually we foul LeBron, who makes one of two free-throws. I scramble on our end for a last desperate shot, but nothing has been going in and this shot is no different. The buzzer goes off. 93–89. They had come back from being down 3–1 in the Finals to a historically successful team. And in the last seconds of Game 7, they beat us on our home floor. I will always give love to Bron and Kyrie for the level they played during the comeback—23 and 2 were special.

In that moment, I stood there by the bench and watched them celebrate. I dapped up Bron, Kyrie, J. R. Smith. I got back to the locker room.

And then everything goes black. I went on autopilot. Not just that night. All of the off-season. I know I worked hard, but **I don't remember a single thing about it.**

You becom[e]
think you ar[e]
in your min[d]
apologi[ze]

e who you
e. Be the best
d and don't
ze for it.

So, what's the lesson of that loss? What can I offer you?

It's really hard to win.

People have asked me with a straight face, "Does the team regret going after seventy-three wins? Did that make you flame out in the Finals?" No. That was an amazing accomplishment, but it *is* bittersweet.

We have the 73-9 poster, a little one in our practice facility. The loneliest banner in the history of the sport. It's got the record and everybody's name on it. I look at it sometimes. It does remind me of the Finals, the loss, but it also reminds me that everybody thought the 72-10 was untouchable. And we got it.

We sustained a high level of basketball for a very, very long time. We maintained that level of focus and performance for nine straight months.

Each year has a different narrative, and I've come to appreciate all of them. **We didn't lose; we got beat, and it was a fight.**

That's the lesson of that year for me: When you get beat, make sure it's a fight.

We stood on a grassy area outside the Hamptons mansion, just the five of us now.

It was June 30, 2016, and me, Andrew, Klay, and Draymond were there to help Kevin Durant understand that we really did want him to come to the Bay. He was a free agent, getting the show from all these teams who wanted him.

The business guys had stayed inside the mansion after their living-room pitch, and now it was just us. People had tried to complicate the idea of him coming to the Warriors. How would I handle a superstar player coming onto the team? Would it threaten my sense of leadership? The better question is, What kind of leader would I be if it did?

What K needed to know from me was more direct: *How did I feel? Did I want him on the team?*

"We want to win," I said. "Think you could help?" As a leader, I needed to know that he was fully committed to what we want to do and how we do it, and if he could answer affirmatively to that, that was all that mattered.

Because the question of adding one of the best players in the league—in the history of the league—to our team was *not* rocket science. The four of us knew who we were as a unit, and here you have a guy who's super-talented and, we discovered, super-motivated to win.

On July 4, when he announced his decision to join Golden State, I was in Hawaii on a family vacation. K tried to call me before he told the world, but with the time difference from the East Coast, I was still asleep by the time he announced. Half the day—and half the news cycle—had passed before I even knew what was going on.

"I thought you were pissed off," K told me later that day. "When you didn't call me back."

"Sorry, man," I said, "that was something else. I didn't know what was going on."

As a leader, it's always got to be about prioritizing the team, prioritizing winning, and understanding that it doesn't diminish my value or my role to have another talented individual coming in to join the movement. It was the start of three great years.

When you begin a new collaboration, you have to remember that everyone is getting used to one another. It's not going to be perfect and it's not necessarily going to be pretty. But you have to be mindful and open up your brain. Think creatively about how to open up space for one another to score. Focus on sharpening your ability to compete. **Build a team identity around trying to win.**

The big picture is that egos come in all shapes and sizes. In every industry, but especially sports, with the competitive nature of what we do, there are public and private conversations around "Whose team is it?" and "Who's the best player on the team?" and "How does this impact legacy?" All of that. I'm just not wired that way.

Focus on your value and how it impacts winning. People talk about setting egos aside, but I don't think that really helps the team. At the end of the day, we all gotta keep our egos. It makes us who we are. It's okay for everybody to bring our healthy egos and best selves to the floor every night.

I want the guy at the locker next to me to think he is the best guy to ever put on a Warriors uniform. As long as he's on my team, that is how I want him to think. My ego is strong enough to handle him having a deep-down belief that he could be better than me. There will be a moment when he will have to be, a moment when I'm slumping or injured or just need to pass the ball off. If his ego is set to 10, he is shot ready for *that* moment.

You become who you think you are. Be the best in your mind and don't apologize for it.

It was the lesson I learned in pickup games in Charlotte: Surround yourself with harder-working people. And that's who Kevin Durant was for me—and who I was for him. We would work out together, maybe once or twice a week—same with Klay. Working on our craft. But there would be times when four of us would be using the four different courts of our practice facility. Each one of us would have his own basket, doing his own work. There would just be this raw energy in there of each of us kinda one-upping each other with how hard we were going. All of us always watching the others to keep the pace we were going at and the intensity that we had. Constantly leveling up. It was such a healthy environment to just get *better*.

    Looking back, I see how we shared an intentionality and professionalism around everything we did. We sharpened one another's game without really talking about it because we were always watching one another. And **nobody wanted to be the weak link.**

It's funny, the different ways you can impact winning. During a game, you can get a kick out of the lengths people will go to defend you. I'll start laughing inside, moving toward half-court and seeing the defender with his face in mine. He's so intent on me that he has absolutely no idea what anyone else is doing behind him. Meanwhile, my teammates are finding open pockets for their own shots or setting up a series of picks that he doesn't even see.

You want to work hard enough to establish yourself so that the threat of what you can do is enough to draw players. **Keep their focus on what you could do, rather than what you're doing.**

Rituals are vital to any team. Not for superstition, but to settle your nerves. They can help you relax so you can focus and enjoy being present in whatever game it is. Game number one, number 82, playoffs, the Finals . . . wherever you are.

For me, it starts with my ankle braces and socks. I put my lefts on before my rights. *Always*. Left-side brace, then right. Left shoe, right shoe. And every year I pick a new song to play for the last three minutes of the drive to the arena. People expect it to be some inspirational track, but one year it was New Edition's "If It Isn't Love." The song—and any ritual—**lets your body and mind know it's time.**

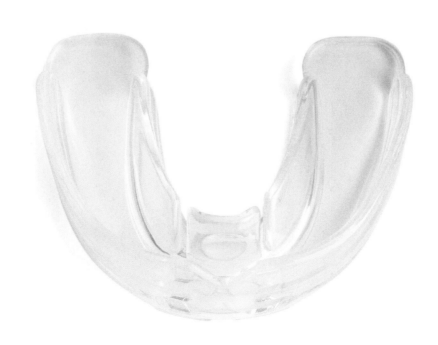

Your loved ones—and maybe strangers—are going to want to give you advice. Make sure you appreciate their support and encouragement, but **set boundaries on their input.** If they haven't done what you're doing, been in the arena, then you really don't want to let them dictate the mechanics or the X's and O's.

My streak of 157 games with a made three-pointer came to a crashing halt in L.A. on November 4, 2016. I went 0-for-10 on threes in a loss against the Lakers.

I was hard on myself in practice the next two days—Saturday and Sunday—but I didn't change my process.

In moments of failure, you have to acknowledge whatever happened so there can be room for growth. But it shouldn't kill your confidence. It's not like I worked any harder than I usually do that weekend between the Lakers game and the Monday game in New Orleans. Instead, I worked with confidence and intentionality: This is going to be a very short downturn, because I know I'm prepared. I was not burdened. I was focused.

Hitting the floor in New Orleans November 7 against the Pelicans, I played free. I didn't have to put any extra pressure on myself. Once I felt the first one go in, I thought, *I'm hot again. One shot is all it takes, no matter how many I've missed before—I'm hot.* That night I made an NBA record of 13 threes.

In moments
have to ac
whatever hap
can be room

of failure, you
knowledge
pened so there
for growth.

June 12, 2017, we were at Oracle—up three games to one in the Finals against the Cavs again. It was Game 5 and, of course, I knew what had happened the year before when we were up three-one.

We had won in 2015 and lost in 2016, so this was our third straight year as one of the last two teams standing. We knew what it felt like to win—but we'd never closed it out on our own floor. I wanted to know what Oracle would feel like the moment the buzzer went off.

That was the motivation. But the nerves were there. Again.

We entered the fourth quarter with a 98–93 lead over the Cavs. Then, with nine minutes left, we increased that lead to 10 points after a pair of free-throws by Draymond.

The last nine minutes of the game felt like a whole week. The win felt so far away, but it was right there in front of us. It just took forever to hear that final horn. It was only when I saw KD kind of break down emotionally across from the bench that I knew. *Oh, we're here*, I thought. *We made it. This is what we all wanted.*

When I say *all*, I don't just mean the team or the coaches. It was everyone in Dub Nation. I'd wanted this for them, here in our home, and the energy in the building did not disappoint. Probably the loudest I've ever heard an arena to this day. To see the fans who stuck with us to the buzzer—the same ones who'd stuck with us 'til the buzzer when we lost? To see all the confetti falling around them?

It was finally the night that Oakland deserved.

With each championship, I felt my public platform getting bigger. I'd been given an incredible opportunity to make a difference. There's pressure that comes with that. You need judgment as you stake your name and voice to a mission. But you lower that pressure when you only align yourself with causes that are authentic to you. I'd grown up watching my parents give back to the community that supported us. My dad set up computer learning centers for middle-school and high-school kids in Charlotte, and he always made sure my siblings and I showed up to help out. We were the same age as those kids, so we fully understood how tangible impact looked.

    It was a model for how I wanted to approach philanthropy and using my platform—**the community I knew, the work I understood, the impact I could see.**

It was the third year of my Under Armour All-American camp, where I invited the top 30 high-school basketball players in the country. (The first two years it was just guys, but after that we were able to expand to the most talented girls in high-school basketball, too. When you know better, you do better.)

I looked around at these kids—most of them taller than me—and I had one thought: *Yo, when I was 16, a junior, I wouldn't have been invited to my own camp.*

What about the kids who are like I was—three-star recruits looking for an opportunity? They deserved a chance to prove themselves and maybe set themselves up to pursue a college scholarship.

That was the start of our first Underrated Tour in 2019. A free, open-invite regional tour for three-star recruits who just love the game like I do. Who find that *joy* in showing up, even when they've been counted out.

The goal is not just to give them a chance to showcase their abilities to coaches and recruiters, but also to enhance their lives in a deeper way. We set them up with gear, and we offer classes detailing what it's like to balance college curriculums and athletics. There's also a seminar on what they need to know as they and their parents navigate a recruiting process that doesn't always have their best interests in mind. I'm also proud that we've been able to give boys and girls the same number of spots.

It's an opportunity to change the lives of late bloomers flying under the radar, kids who need to see what they can do and be grateful for who they are becoming, instead of just comparing themselves to someone else. **I know all about being a late bloomer.**

Fatherhood will help you with perspective. I'm not talking about the dreamy storybook scenario of **finally realizing what is important.** I am talking about your kids telling you what matters. I learned early that it didn't matter how many points I scored or whose record I broke—what game we won or lost—they did not care. When I come home, I'm Dad, and what children want is for you to match the energy they give you. Leave the stress of work out of that relationship and seize on the opportunity of walking in that door and starting fresh. Because they really don't care, and it's not a little kid's job to care about your role outside of being the parent they can count on. Instead, find out something that they care about and study it as if you were prepping for a client meeting. Whether it's My Little Pony or types of airplanes—learn their language so they can practice having real conversations about the things that matter to them.

    I know that boundaries between work and home have never been flimsier. Phones, Zooms, weekend work—we've all gotten used to it. In my work, I've had to practice those boundaries my whole career, because sometimes I'm on road trips for 10 days at a time. The days blur together if you're not careful. The trick is to be 100 percent present wherever you are.

CENTER

FOUR FACTORS	
EFG%	00.0
TO%	00.0
OREB%	00.0
FT RATE	00.0

LOS ANGELES TEAM STATS

AST	00.0	BLK	00.0	2P%	
OREB	00.0	TO	00.0	3P%	00.0
DREB	00.0	POT	00.0	FG%	00.0
STL	00.0	PITP	00.0	FT%	00.0

THE FLOOR	MIN	PTS	REB	AST	STL	BLK	FGM/FGA	3PM/3PA	FLS
J. MCGEE	00	00	00	00	00	00	00/00	00/00	00
K. KUZMA	00	00	00	00	00	00	00/00	00/00	00
L. JAMES	00	00	00	00	00	00	00/00	00/00	00
D. GREEN	00	00	00	00	00	00	00/00	00/00	00
R. RONDO	00	00	00	00	00	00	00/00	00/00	00

CHASE CENTER   WELCOME

STEPHEN
CURRY

CHASE CENTER   WELCOME

CHASE CENTER   CHASE CENTER

CURRENT TOTAL: $20,000   CLE 100   IND 100   Q4 17

It was surreal seeing my son Canon sitting on my dad's lap at his first game on March 31, 2019. Our young wolf, eight months and growing up with the same privilege of going to the games that I had. I want to create the same kind of memories for him—but the game was also a beautiful moment for me and my dad. I could see in that image— Canon on Dad's lap—how far I'd come from watching him play, and how far he'd come from being a player and a father to being a granddad and a young patriarch for a growing family. He is not a prideful man, but in moments like that I can see it—his deep sense of contentment and pride in what he's inspired me and my brother Seth to do in the league and in our lives.

As you start to grow into being a veteran, you have a role in helping your team manage change. Even when you don't want to face it yourself. One of those changes for me was the news that the Warriors were leaving Oracle for Chase Center at the end of the 2018–2019 season.

I'd put off taking my first tour of Chase Center as long as I could. Ayesha came with me, and we put on the same hard hats and bright-yellow safety vests as the crew doing the tour. They'd been working on this site two years since breaking ground, and they were all really excited to show me the work. I tried to mirror that enthusiasm back to them, show them I appreciated all the long hours they'd spent building what was an undeniably perfect place to play basketball.

Ayesha couldn't even look at me because she could sense what I was feeling, no matter how many times I said "Wow, that's crazy" or "That's nuts" with my hands clasped tight in front of me or behind my back. As beautifully designed and state-of-the-art as Chase Center was, it still felt empty—we'd already poured everything we were as a team into Oracle.

I exhaled in the car, alone with Ayesha. "I was just *there*," I said, low and quiet. It wasn't the spiritual event for me that I thought it would be. It wasn't home yet. Not *ours*.

That was something I would need to figure out, not just for me but for the team. **Veterans, as much as we hold on to the experiences that forged us, sometimes need to shepherd people through the unknown.**

As we were preparing to leave Oracle for Chase Center at the end of the 2018–2019 season, I wanted to shine a light on the support system I had and the people that came before me. The legends that paved the way for me to be able to do what I'm doing—the guys who have their jerseys in the rafters.

I was the OG of my team, and the only one still there from '09. To honor Warriors history, I asked that the team wear throwback jerseys from the "We Believe" era as we said goodbye to the arena. When we saw the uniforms in our lockers, that's when it got real to me that we were really leaving Oracle. I put it on, and when I caught sight of myself in a mirror, it wasn't that memories came flooding back, but gratitude for these 10 years.

We hit the court and the fans exploded, the ones who'd believed in that team, and whose respect and belief we'd worked hard to earn in these past years. Oakland will always be ride or die.

Part of the last five home games, I picked people to honor by wearing their Warriors jersey pregame: BD (Baron Davis), Andris Biedriņš, Stack (Stephen Jackson), Tim Hardaway, and, on the last night, Monta Ellis. Monta was someone the narrative said was supposed to be my enemy, which sounds ridiculous now. Monta came out of high school and found himself having to lead this team we both love. He is beloved, and it was only right to have him, and that history of leadership, represented at our last regular-season night at Oracle, a night we would win the Western Conference, punching our ticket to the Finals once again.

I have a picture the team took with the fans after we lost the Finals in 2019. We'd lost to the Raptors, the team I'd watched my father play for all those times with my brother Seth in Toronto. This was truly our last night in Oracle.

From the locker room, we'd heard the fans filing out, chanting "Warriors" for the last time in that arena, the oldest one in the NBA. There were about 70 holdouts, fans who were having trouble saying goodbye. Just like us. We went back out to meet them, and we all took a photo together.

We lost, but there were so many amazing memories—lessons and experiences—that we had in that building. **So we celebrated. It was the right way to go out.**

In transitions like that, and even in losses, you have an opportunity to lead your people through it, down through the valley, and back up to the top of the mountain.

There are moments when a leader's job is to leave the past behind. To start a new history.

Part 3

Veteran

Stretching Your Prime

A veteran brings all their years of playing to each game—the wins and losses. You don't have that blessing of being naïve anymore. You know from experience that things can and will go wrong in crucial moments.

Veterans can lose their confidence trying to be too deliberate and careful because they know the stakes so well—they know the pitfalls, the possibilities of error. That's where you lean into the amnesia you practiced as a rookie. The stubbornness that nothing before the shot you're about to take matters. **Remember the beginner's mind.** Nothing exists but right now.

This is the moment that matters.

The next one's going in.

"How does it feel to be the oldest guy on the team?"

This was probably the question I was most asked at training camp before the 2019–2020 season. It was as if reporters had a shortcut-key that September to type out "Curry, who at 31 is the oldest player on the roster . . ." I tried to be transparent: "Has it sunk in yet? No. Have people been reminding me? Yes. Hopefully I'm wise beyond my years but still youthful in what I can do on the floor."

My main focus that year was leading the team through the challenges and opportunities of a new roster. We'd not only lost Kevin Durant, an all-around all-time great player, but we also said goodbye to Andre Iguodala and Shaun Livingston, two veterans with irreplaceable basketball IQ. Klay was out after surgery on the ACL he tore in Game 6 against the Raptors. That left me as the old guy, helping everyone get used to the Warriors' new home at Chase Center.

Just before our first preseason game, Draymond and I talked about settling into our new digs. "Man, this is the first game at Chase Center ever," he said. "You gotta do something crazy."

"What you mean?"

"You gotta like . . ." He thought for a second. "First time you touch the ball, you gotta like shoot from half-court or something." I laughed, and he gave me that look. He was dead serious.

Obviously, I wanted to play well my first game there, but establishing our undeniable ownership of the space hadn't occurred to me—making the first shot to show the world that this was our space. But Draymond was right.

"Yeah," I said, smiling. "Let me put my stamp on this arena."

"That's right," he said, gassing me up. "That's right."

We got the tip, and I came across half-court. *Okay,* I thought, striding maybe about two or three feet in, and I just flung it.

Airball.

And it went out of bounds. I started laughing, and I looked over at Coach, who didn't know the plan. Poor guy saw the jump ball happen and the next thing he knows, he's seeing me flinging it 40 feet.

It broke the ice on the arena for all of us. We were there to have fun. **"Welcome to Chase," I said aloud to myself and to everyone there.**

The deeper I get into my career, the more important it is that I have control over my breathing. It is the smallest detail that expands into everything I do. It is the secret weapon; one no one can see me do when I utilize it on the court.

The vets I play with need the reminder to breathe, too. The stakes are too high when you're older. People are looking at you to see if you've plateaued, and sometimes you get a little fed up with other people's learning curves. So, you start yelling at a ref—whether or not they had it coming—or throwing your mouthguard. Or you make a new hire feel small rather than showing them their potential to learn from a mistake. **Success will never come without stress, but controlled breathing can help you train your response to that stress.**

The first year at Chase Center was rough. We lost that 2019–2020 opening night against the Clippers, went on the road, and then came back to Chase for the fourth game of the season. Our opponent was Phoenix. It was only our second game at Chase. In the third quarter, a 6'10" center named Aron Baynes tried to block a shot and I tripped over him. He lost his balance and landed on the back of my hand.

    I got up, shook it off, but realized **something was really wrong.** I'd broken the second metacarpal

of my hand. Two days later, I had surgery to reset the break, then a follow-up a month later to remove the pins. I have two beautiful scars on my left hand, part of me now.

My trainer Brandon Payne admitted that this was the most worrying of all my injuries—every other one had involved a muscle or ligament, but this was a bone. What scared me was the numbness that came with the injury. It would take seven months for full feeling to come back to two fingers on my left hand.

I was out for four months. Because my rehab was down in Southern California, I was away from the team for the most part. But in that time, I was determined to stay a leader and resource for the team. When you can't be present for your team, it challenges you in a different way: How are you checking in on guys when you're not actually present? How do you make sure everybody's maintaining the team culture in the locker room?

If you pay attention to those things, you realize how much your voice and your presence can carry even if you're not out there playing. **Notice all the little nuances of connecting with your teammates.** It's about making sure that everybody, from the star player down to the fifteenth guy, feels valuable and important to the process of winning.

Unfortunately, that year we were bad. That's just true. It was a full-on sprint for me to get back out there on the floor. Around the new year, I got back into a nice routine of at least coming in the building. Chase didn't feel like home yet. I had only managed to play two games there, and though I'd worked to stay close to the team, I was still anticipating a reintroduction to the fan base and the new environment at Chase Center.

So, when I finally came back for the March 5, 2020, game against the Raptors, I was the new kid getting ready for the first day of school when everyone else had been there for months. Our record at the time was horrible; we were the worst team in the league. Even if we weren't playing for anything as a team because of our record, I love hooping and getting out there. It also helped to get an amazing reception from the fans. I hadn't been out that long, but the fans made it clear that I'd been out long enough to be missed. It was a balm to feel the love.

As a veteran, I was learning to model accepting that love. I always had the gratitude, but now I wanted to show people how to accept love and still be humble.

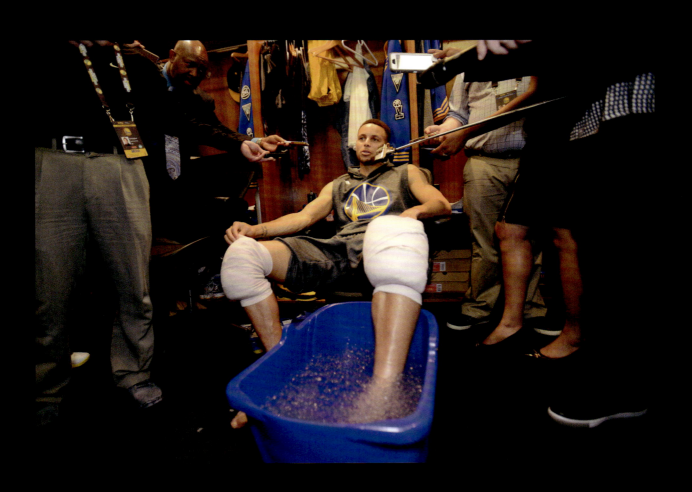

Remember
and grace y
on the c

he patience
ou needed
ome-up.

Life will humble you anyway if you don't do it yourself. I missed my first two shots, but then started to get comfortable. I faked out Patrick McCaw to get a bucket, but what matters to what you and I are discussing is that the shot came late in the 24-second clock, and I honestly just flung it up to beat the buzzer. Any shooter knows, sometimes the way to get on track, when you're searching for rhythm or when things don't feel all the way right, is to put yourself in a position where you literally *can't* overthink things. When the clock is running low and you don't have any choice *but* to shoot the ball, your mind radically simplifies things. You're operating on pure impulse with no thought beyond, "Ugh, I'll just shoot it."

Those are the best shots. **A clear mind. Simple focus.** And sometimes it even goes in.

I smiled so wide. Just back to having fun.

But that wasn't my favorite play of that first game. This was:

I ran through the paint and caught a pass right in front of our bench. I pump-faked and two defenders flew past me—I sidestepped with a quick dribble and slung the ball—with the hand that I *broke*, thank you—behind my back to Andrew Wiggins. He caught it and finished.

I didn't just feel like my left hand was back—I felt my creativity come back, that flair and beauty and sense of wonder that defined Warriors basketball. I played decent that game, still getting used to Chase, but we lost in the last minute or two. The game mattered, though, because it reminded me how much fun I could have in that environment—the same as I can have on any court anywhere. The night showed me that all I put into the game, everything I do to be out there and available to play, was still worth it. I needed that reward at the end of a long rehab stint to get reenergized to play.

And then . . . the league shut down.

Starting March 11, 2020, the NBA canceled its schedule in response to the Covid-19 pandemic. That summer, the league reopened in "the bubble," a closed facility in Florida's Walt Disney World, to play the last eight games of the season and the playoffs. Twenty-two out of the thirty teams were asked to participate, with the bottom eight already eliminated from playoff contention.

With a record of only 15 wins in 50 games, we were 30th of 30. Last place. The Warriors did not get an invite. Not going to Disney World meant there would be another seven or eight months before the new season started and I could play again.

It was also an end to the schedule that we have to live by in the NBA. This felt different from the NBA lockout when I was a newlywed, or doing the day-to-day precision rehab work I needed to return from injury. I was adrift. It was the lowest point in my career.

Ever since I was a kid watching my dad play, and then into my adulthood, I've thought about life in the cycle of basketball's seasons: You've got preseason, the regular season before the All-Star break, the All-Star break until the playoffs, and then the playoffs, and finally, the off-season. That's how I see the year—the way that I have learned to compartmentalize my energy and prioritize my life.

And now it was gone. The pause was jarring, but I wanted to take advantage of that time to focus on getting stronger and even more efficient with every single movement. I was going to be coming back at age 33. **This, I remember thinking, is an opportunity.**

God has a way of prepping you to meet the moment, and I was proud to watch my wife rise to the challenge that the pandemic brought to our community. Ayesha has always had a passion for ending childhood hunger, and through the years I watched her work with organizations to learn how to most effectively fulfill that mission. Together in 2019, we decided to invest our time and love into creating a sort of village for kids, supporting the community that supports us.

We assembled a team to develop Eat. Learn. Play., a program that gives kids what they need to have a happy, healthy childhood: nutritious meals, quality reading resources, and safe spaces to be active.

Little did we know that we'd have the ability to jump into action within three months of being an operational foundation. We were set up perfectly to spring into action when Covid hit in March 2020. So many kids rely on schools for meal programs—breakfast and lunch—that were cut away as quick as the snap of a finger. We had to pivot dramatically, but we were able to do meal distribution and reopen certain restaurants to get people back to work. **The fact that we could meet the demand that was there—that was all God.**

Like I say, preparation is everything. We're up to 20 million meals distributed, and we're forever grateful to have been a part of a critical response to a historic crisis.

When we were trying to figure out what equips a kid to reach their full potential, we came up with those three necessities: Eating, learning, and playing. Of the three, literacy was especially crucial to me.

My mom is an educator so I've always understood how important it is to give kids access to books that are culturally relevant and age-appropriate. Making reading fun is *the* key to unlocking a kid's ability to be successful in their academic journeys.

My mom is a driving force behind that. She founded the Montessori school that I went to from first through sixth grades. She was also a teacher, and the principal. Back then, I couldn't have escaped her if I wanted to, and now I'm just trying to keep up with her as an educator.

Maybe the most powerful and transformative thing we do at **Eat. Learn. Play.** is tell kids what we're going to do for them and then execute it. A promise fulfilled means more to them than any pledge of a gazillion dollars that gets headlines.

We cover all operational expenses for the foundation so that every dollar that comes in is 100 percent going directly back into the community. As I write this, we are now working with the Oakland Unified School District to infuse more than $50 million into the school system over the next four years. That's where kids go to eat, learn, and play every single day. We have a real opportunity there to meet them where they are.

Take your opportunity to be of service. My advice is to start by making a difference in your immediate community, with a specific and clear impact in mind. Then develop a strategy around that goal.

If I'd known that the January 3, 2021, game at home against Portland was going to be my new career high, I might have done something different with my hair.

This was the Covid-shortened season, which had only started a few days before Christmas. We'd already had some bad losses, including a loss to the Trail Blazers on New Year's Day. Now it was the rematch, and there was talk about Portland's Dame Lillard being the new rising star and the Warriors' era of dominance ending.

That game I went nuts. An out-of-body experience where all I needed was a split second of daylight and the ball was going up and going in. **I felt that sense of meditative calm I'm always hoping for where I don't have to even think.**

I scored a career-high 62 points. It was a reminder to the world: We are still right here.

As you get older, you appreciate more and more the foundation that family gives you. Everyone isn't as lucky as me, I know, but for me, my parents have been the foundation to everything I've done. Family structures can change, take on new shapes, and maybe even split apart. Circumstances—*life*—can force you to reimagine all your relationships. Even so, you can still provide that support for one another. My parents got divorced in 2021, and it was initially hard for me even if I didn't fully reckon with it. But maturity and wisdom come from all the things that you go through, and I came to see that rethinking of my family as a blessing. What lessons could I bring into my own marriage to make it even stronger? How could I convey appreciation to each of my parents separately for pouring their love and confidence into me throughout my life? Through the years, I've trained myself to **see the opportunity in the hurdle.** And now I also see the beauty.

These are the moments I love: Out of 82 games, there's probably 15 to 20 moments where you feel a direct correlation to the work you did that summer. I will look at Q with the other trainers on the sideline and point at him.

I worked on one shot last year, a little scoop shot that I had never really worked on before but had just started doing in the middle of the 2014 season. It kind of became a staple.

But suddenly I was awful at it. I was short, long. Couldn't make it. I have to have the shot in my arsenal as an option for closing drives. I'm not going above the rim to dunk on anybody, so I need a shot with a quick release and high trajectory that I can get up before some giant tries to block it.

That season I missed the shot six straight times over the course of several games. I went to morning workout after that spell and told Q, "I'm really struggling with this one."

We started working on it with real intensity as he tried to fix my balance. We disregarded every other part of my game and just concentrated on that one shot, but with **game-speed mentality.** The next game I made one and I pointed at Q on the bench, right in the middle of the game. When things aren't working I need feedback from my coaches to get fresh perspective and solve some puzzles. Sometimes it feels like chess. Sometimes it's a little like whack-a-mole.

Back when I was a rookie, I could go through all my routines and play a game—then wake up the next morning just ready to go. Now, it's different. I start preparing for the next day as soon as the current day's work is done. From diet to sleep to recovery strategies to film study, there's an endless cycle of preparing for the next game, and it starts way earlier than I ever had to as a rookie.

 I'm writing this to you at 3:40 P.M. on a Friday. I'll play at 5:30 P.M. on Saturday, and about two hours ago I started the process to get ready for the game. In my head. From 4:30 to 7:30 it will be strictly kids and family and dinner. Then after their bedtime routines, from 8:30 to 10:00 I have time carved out for body work. Then it's a nightcap with my wife and sleep.

It took some getting used to, being the veteran in the room. Last summer I met a new teammate for the first time. "Yo, I was in eighth grade when you won your MVP award," he said.

"My first or second?" was the only answer. But it's true: When we won our first championship, a lot of my teammates were in elementary school.

It's hilarious, but it makes me feel good. Because **I know I'm still in my prime.** I can laugh about the distance I've already traveled because I don't see an end.

Understand that the next generation will test your leadership. Daily. They are going through all these experiences for the first time, some you encountered and learned through, and some that are completely foreign to you. In the way that the generation before me was able to disappear in the off-season with no camera phones or reports on how their private training sessions were going, the generation after mine faces different pressures. **Remember the patience and grace you needed on the come-up.** Offer it to others now.

As young players, we had to build a championship DNA into our team; as vets now, we have a responsibility to maintain it and pass it on. I know, vets have enough to worry about with ourselves and our own performance—but let me tell you how we **make time and space to motivate our younger players:**

Imagine coming into our facility. There's a little corner section of the enormous practice complex that's our space to go over film. The scene is like any college or high-school gym—down to us rolling out the fold-up chairs and a TV on wheels. One of the most state-of-the-art arenas in America, and that's how we watch film every day.

That's where most of our mentoring conversations happen—when we're watching the film, noting where we execute well and when we don't.

Me, Draymond, and Andre Iguodala—we were the main spokespeople at these sessions when Iggy was still playing. Obviously, this also happens with Coach Kerr and the staff, but as veterans we had a license to offer full honesty and transparency. It could be as straightforward as me saying, "The last two first quarters were rough—we're giving up way too many points, and when you don't start well, you're giving the other team reason to keep their foot on the gas." Or it could be very Draymondesque, a passionate five-minute monologue that gets everybody's attention.

We also give pointers in our group text—motivational speeches and messages from some of the team leaders. Pregame, it will pop up on your phone. Draymond might have a word for us on what tonight's game means, then I'll chime in with some broader notes to build our confidence. I focus on reminding people that we're headed in the right direction, even if it's one of the moments when we have to turn a setback into a learning lesson.

The Warriors went into the 2021–2022 season with high hopes but no idea what it would be like for us all to play together. We had a mixed bag of young and old players. In the latter camp, obviously me and Draymond were the two members of the corps trying to lead the charge, with Klay out for the first half of the year.

That combination of veterans and new guys can be hard. As vets, you are trying to be open to marry a new team's identity with the winning methods that you know from experience. There is an inherent conflict there, where the idea of who you are as a team is one thing, but the reality of who you are as a group of individuals is different.

In training camp, I was experimenting, getting a sense of people's skills and potential for growth, while making sure I didn't communicate in a way that made anyone worry they were already falling short. When the season started, I worried that we had still not ironed out the kinks. We were still growing, learning about one another—about who we were as a team—on the fly.

And within that identity crisis, we started 18-2, a winning record that was unheard-of for an age-range team like ours.

We just had to keep it going.

December 14, 2021, at the Garden.

Setting the NBA record for career three-pointers was definitely the goal, I just didn't know when it was going to happen.

Shooting at a high volume with high efficiency is my standard. The week before December 14, I was struggling mightily on the efficiency part because the record was in my head. I was too focused on what the record-breaking moment was gonna feel like. Of course, I remembered watching the game on February 10, 2011, when Ray Allen broke Reggie Miller's record at home in Boston. I can still see the shot he hit—a deep three in the first quarter—and how amazing it was that Reggie Miller was broadcasting the game, there to pass the torch. "Two thousand five hundred sixty-one . . ." he said, stretching it out to show the magnitude of the new record. Then they stopped the game to celebrate the milestone. It was just surreal to think that I was going to be in that position.

I went into the game on the 14th needing *two* to break Ray Allen's career three-point record of 2,973. How crazy is it that it was at the Garden? The Mecca of basketball history and where it all began for me. I tied the record with a three-pointer before the two-minute mark. Then Draymond passed down low to Andrew Wiggins. I went back to the three-point line. Wiggs passed to me, and the rest is history.

To do it at the Garden, and in front of Ray, in front of Reggie, and in front of my family, was magical. I still reel from the emotions of that. I was very grateful to have Ray and Reggie there at center court, 8,505 three-pointers between us.

Coach Kerr made an observation that night: In that game alone, our team and the Knicks made 82 attempts at three-pointers. It showed how much the league had changed since I started. He often reminds me that he had the best three-point percentage in history, but he always jokes that it's because he was shooting wide-open shots—two or three a game—versus me trying to shoot 12 threes a game with everyone out to stop me. I was proud to be part of a tradition. **But I also took pride in changing the game.**

2,9

People look back on that 2021–2022 season and focus on the beginning and the end—a championship. They miss the middle. We came out of the gates running, with everything clicking. For the new guys, that seemed like a natural result of just being on the team. At that point, we had won three championships and being a Warrior meant something. If you're new to the team, there's a weight that comes with putting on that jersey—a pressure to prove you belong there. But they'd studied me and Draymond, and now they were playing alongside us. They probably thought, *Of course we're winning*.

Then we weren't. After that streak of 18 wins and two losses, we hit a rocky point. Suddenly, we were far from that type of a winning team—what Warriors were supposed to be—for about three months. We had gotten to know one another while we were winning. We didn't know who we were once we started losing.

My own doubt started to creep in, which is dangerous. When I feel a little vulnerable like that, the expanse of a season begins to stretch out before me. Eighty-two games is a very long run.

Veterans and new guys face different challenges, but the results can be the same: **overthinking and freezing up.** The new guys get in their heads wondering how they lost something that was working— either looking for someone to blame or feeling they have been revealed as the impostor who is bringing everyone else down. Us veterans are having flashbacks—remembering how hard it is to win and the pain of driving home after a devastating loss.

Either way—vet or new guy, MVP or rookie—that loss of confidence makes you too careful, so afraid to mess up that you don't take the shot in a crucial situation. You override your instinct.

So, what could the veterans offer the younger members of the team, when we knew better than anyone how hard it is to win a game in the NBA? To win just *one* game, let alone our goal of winning a championship?

Win just *one* game.

The first thing we did was take big goals and turn them into bite-sized pieces. "Accomplishable things" became our guiding principle— little wins that got us closer to an end goal that we were no longer going to talk about so much. Because if we kept talking about the end goal, it put too much pressure on everything that we did on a daily basis.

So, we took a step back and asked, "What are those bite-sized pieces that we can obsess over?"

How can we go into *this* game and not foul more than 15 times? Or not turn the ball over more than 10 times *tonight*? How do we keep *this* team under a certain point total defensively?

I'm speaking to you in terms of basketball, but you can take this into life. Don't try to win the season. Win the week. Now, our team has incorporated this into our everyday approach, no matter what our record is. For instance, if we're playing three games over seven days, we can focus on winning two so we can claim a winning record for the week. These smaller wins create the little moments of motivation and celebration you'll need to get through the tough parts of your season.

I obsess over those "small" types of goals—which keep me in a "one game at a time" mentality—it almost tricks you, one small goal at a time, into covering all the details that it takes to win at the highest level. We were becoming a championship team by not talking about it; we simply enjoyed the process of getting better every day.

It started with some self-talk down the stretch in the fourth quarter in Game 3 of the Denver series in April 2022. We got a stop. A minute left.

Put 'em to sleep, I told myself. Put 'em to sleep.

As a dad, there is no greater accomplishment some nights than bedtime. Getting the job done.

We gotta put this to bed, I thought.

I made a layup, then put my hands together in the "night-night" gesture, just for me.

Put 'em to sleep, I told myself. *Put 'em to sleep.*

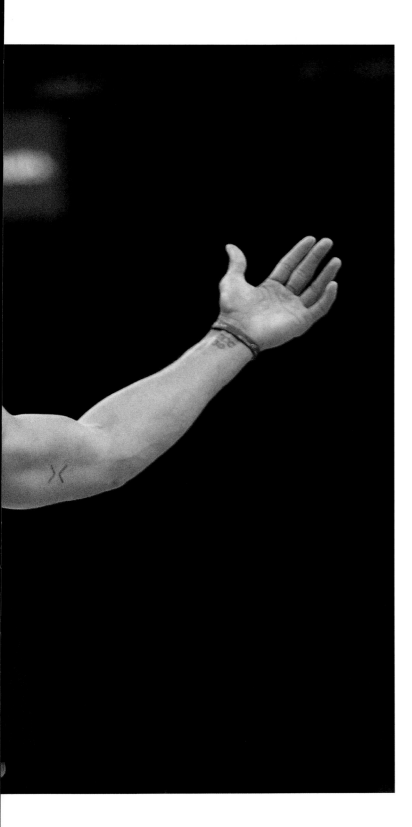

In Boston, down 2–1.

It was Game 4 of the Finals in 2022. We pretty much knew if we lost, it was over. The Boston crowd had been booing and cussing Draymond all night. And I took that personally, too. It's easy for fans to get loud and abusive like that when their team is ahead.

I made a shot in the first quarter and started yelling at the entire arena. Just trying to bring a different level of energy: **"We are here. Yeah! It's a different day!"**

It was a different expression of competitiveness than I'd ever had—flexing and waving my arms to be seen. If they—their team, their crowd—were challenging us to meet their energy and fire, we were going to exceed it. Usually, as a team we rely on Draymond to bring that fire throughout the course of the season, so it probably makes sense that Draymond tells me this game is his pick for the biggest moment of my career.

I was just trying to win the game.

As a veteran you begin to understand that certain moments require a different level of performance. It's about that balance: You don't want a win so bad that you get in your own way and the pressure sends you spiraling in the wrong direction. Even in a hostile environment, you still gotta show up and play. But sometimes that killer instinct has to come out.

I cried after the horn of Game 6. We'd won our fourth championship. All that emotion from the last few frustrating years came flowing out in ugly tears. You carry that emotion with you all the time, even through all those little wins. Everything you pour into the work sticks with you, every detail, every teammate you checked on, everybody you prayed for when they had an injury. All the years of trying to fill in the right pieces and the right guys, while also thanking God every day that you get to play this game at the highest level. As the OG, you carry that with you until it's something you don't even realize you're carrying.

    And then you win. When it happens, hold on to that feeling. I can place myself right back there when I want to, and it's a beautiful feeling. **Let the memory motivate you to get back there when you feel so far away from it.** Run it back and do it again.

Had we kept winning through the regular season of 2021–22, and not dealt with any rockiness until playoff time, I'm pretty sure things would have turned out differently. Without the bumps along the way, we wouldn't have had the chance to learn who we were as a team when things go bad. It's important to make the most of obstacles and setbacks, no matter when they come. Adversity reveals who you have become and who you have yet to become. What a gift to find at the back end of your career—**another chance to discover who you are and who you can be.**

I don't usually take my four championship rings anywhere. The Finals, MVP, and All-Star trophies—it all stays in the office. But I brought three rings with me to the 2022 championship parade in San Francisco. In fact, I brought every NBA trophy I had onto the float, putting each member of my extended family in charge of one.

At one point they put every piece of hardware in my hand, with a cigar in my mouth. Going down Market Street in a parade after a championship that nobody thought we would win? That's gold.

A parade is an odd moment that mixes a healthy ego-tripping alongside intense feelings of the most selfless gratitude. It lets you stunt a little bit—you are literally being paraded down the street to let people know what you've accomplished. But it's also a chance to thank the people that make it happen: your teammates, the fans, and your family, all of us celebrating this collective achievement together. The parade is a public display of a constant reality: We always show up for one another. We don't ride on floats all the time—but **every day is a private parade of quiet, persistent love, connection, gratitude, and celebration.** Without that foundation, I don't know where I would be.

Every season presents a different challenge.

After winning four championships in seven seasons, we entered the 2022–2023 season knowing that if we didn't win a championship this time, it would be seen by some as a failed season.

In the first round of playoffs that season we were up against Sacramento, and we just didn't play well in Game 6. We let a 3–2 series lead become a tie when we should have closed it out at home. They outhustled us.

I felt like the energy was not in the right place, so I had a talk with the team before film. It's been said that I "delivered a message," but all I talked about was the importance of confidence. We had to believe that we are the team that is capable of winning *this game*. I said that anybody who gets on the team bus to Sacramento is telling me they're fully committed to doing whatever it takes to win.

It's a fair question to ask: "Why should you need a speech when you're in the playoffs on a team that has the résumé we had?" But leadership tests you and challenges you in a lot of different ways. I am not one for speeches—I leave that to coaches and Draymond. But I was going to lose sleep if I didn't say what I needed to say before we went to war in Game 7.

I scored 50 points in that game, 30 in the second half, but we were battling it out as a team. We were defying the odds to still play at this high level when people were counting us out. We won, but then lost to the Lakers in six in the conference semifinals. But we got on the bus and **went into battle, fully prepared.** That was a win.

Joy has stayed with me as the guiding light and motivation, but only because I've safeguarded it. I know how important it is to keep that flame lit so it can fire the work.

When we're on the road, we get optional shooting times. Everybody goes in to get their 30 minutes of work in. And every time, the second right before, I think, *Here we go. Okay, lock in.* Once that first one goes in, the 30 minutes fly by. **Focus, intention, pleasure—my mind clears.**

Change t

he game.

Last Saturday night, after the kids' bedtime, I threw on a hoodie and went out to our backyard court, my dogs following me. It's cold at night here in Northern California, even in summer. Nothing like where I grew up in Charlotte. We have a lot of trees by the house, and as a light breeze moved the oaks and evergreens, I shot the ball. Over and over again. This moment was what I was trying to get to as I retrained my shot 20 years ago in my parents' backyard. This pure joy. I didn't realize I was out there for about 30 minutes—just hooping.

    This afternoon, someone asked me if I was still happy playing basketball, and words failed me. So, I got out my phone and cued up the app of our security cameras. I showed them footage from last Saturday night, me on the court with the dogs. "I want you to see this," I said, "because it captures the pure joy of having the ball in my hand." They leaned over to watch the film. In black-and-white it was as basic as it could possibly be: I dribbled, rose, and shot one ball after another. Bounce. Shot. Swish. **Joy at its highest.**

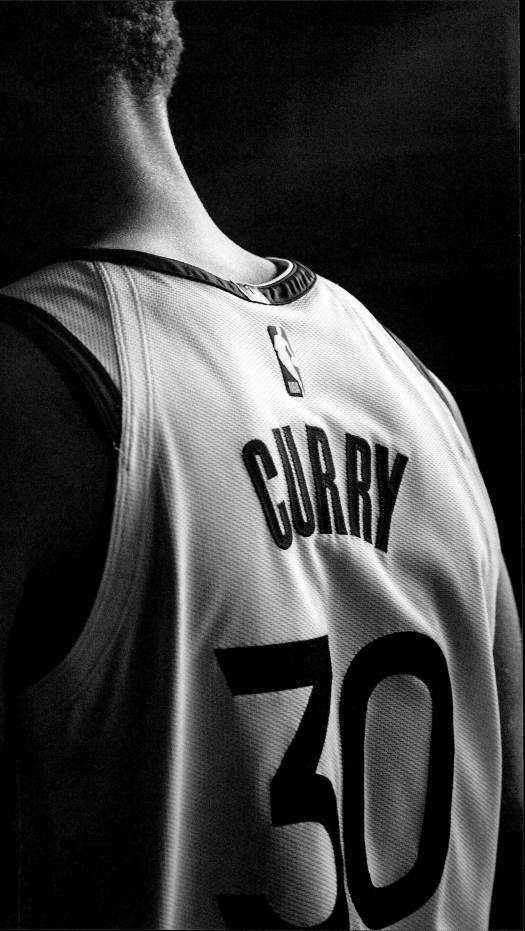

As I move into the tail end of my career, I have confidence that I can continue to thrive. But the questions come: "Are you thinking about retirement?"

I do think about it, but perhaps not in the way they think I do. There is a timeline, but it's not a source of dread. It's a gift. The gift is that the timeline gives me more motivation for the *now.* To take advantage of every opportunity and edge that I have. Because of course I know the ball will stop bouncing eventually. But not yet. **The gift of the timeline is that it keeps me in the moment.**

In a game, I look at the shot clock on each possession to understand how much time I have. The clock is there to tell you whether you've got to press the issue. But as the game goes on, as you get more experienced, you understand that the clock isn't just about time. The clock determines the pace you need to play.

It can make you move faster and decide quicker, but there will be times when you need to work with the clock in a different way, to slow things down and pace yourself.

You can't slow down time, but you can value it. Make it purposeful.

I love doing what I get to do. And I am not arrogant enough to think that I won't miss it. In the meantime, I want to get everything I can out of it, shot ready 'til the end.

    You do the same.

Acknowledgments

Let me express my gratitude to the people who helped get this book off the ground, including my teams at 30Ink (Tiffany and Suresh) and Unanimous Media (EP and KMK). We didn't get here without our partners at UTA, Byrd Leavell and Albert Lee. The most instrumental teammates were Kevin Carr O'Leary, Khristopher "Squint" Sandifer, Getty Images, and all the incredible photographers featured within the pages. To the people who have always been in my corner, a special thank-you goes out to the NBA and the Warriors.

And to my family . . . Ayesha, Riley, Ryan, Canon, and Caius: I love you.

Image Credits

Pages XVIII–XIX © Khristopher "Squint" Sandifer
Page XX © Khristopher "Squint" Sandifer
Pages 4–5 © Khristopher "Squint" Sandifer
Page 6 © Khristopher "Squint" Sandifer
Page 7 © Khristopher "Squint" Sandifer
Page 9 © Khristopher "Squint" Sandifer
Page 11 (top) © Khristopher "Squint" Sandifer
Page 11 (bottom) © Devin Allen
Page 12 © Noah Graham
Page 13 (top) © Noah Graham
Page 13 (bottom) © Khristopher "Squint" Sandifer
Page 15 © Noah Graham
Pages 16–17 © Devin Allen
Pages 18–19 © Khristopher "Squint" Sandifer
Page 22 (top) © Khristopher "Squint" Sandifer
Page 22 (bottom) © Khristopher "Squint" Sandifer
Pages 24–25 © Devin Allen
Page 27 © Khristopher "Squint" Sandifer
Pages 28–29 © Getty Images
Pages 30–31 © Khristopher "Squint" Sandifer
Page 32 from Curry family archive
Page 33 from Curry family archive
Pages 34–35 © Khristopher "Squint" Sandifer
Pages 36–37 © Devin Allen
Page 38 Courtesy of Sonya Curry
Pages 40–41 © Devin Allen
Page 43 (top) © Devin Allen
Page 43 (bottom) © Devin Allen
Pages 44–45 © Khristopher "Squint" Sandifer
Page 46 © Khristopher "Squint" Sandifer
Page 47 © Khristopher "Squint" Sandifer
Page 49 Courtesy of Sonya Curry
Page 50 © Devin Allen
Page 53 © Khristopher "Squint" Sandifer
Pages 54–55 © John Walder
Pages 56–57 © Noah Graham
Page 58 © 2022 NBAE (Photo by Garrett Ellwood/NBAE via Getty Images)
Pages 60–61 © Khristopher "Squint" Sandifer
Page 64 © Khristopher "Squint" Sandifer
Page 65 © Devin Allen
Pages 66–67 © Khristopher "Squint" Sandifer
Page 68 © Devin Allen
Page 69 © Devin Allen
Page 71 Courtesy of Sonya Curry
Pages 72–73 © John Walder
Page 74 © John Walder
Page 75 © John Walder
Pages 76–77 © Illustration by No Ideas with Nicolas Ardeley
Pages 78–79 © Khristopher "Squint" Sandifer
Page 81 Courtesy of Sonya Curry
Page 83 Courtesy of Sonya Curry
Page 85 © Adobe Stock
Page 87 © Photo by Kavin Mistry/Getty Images
Page 89 © Photo by Kevin C. Cox/Getty Images
Page 90 © Khristopher "Squint" Sandifer
Page 93 © Photo by Gregory Shamus/

Getty Images
Page 94 © Photo by Streeter Lecka/Getty Images
Pages 96–97 © Khristopher "Squint" Sandifer
Page 99 (top) © John Walder
Page 99 (bottom) © John Walder
Page 100 (top) © John Walder
Page 100 (bottom) © John Walder
Page 102 © 2009 NBAE (Photo by Angie Lovelace/NBAE via Getty Images)
Page 103 © Photo by Ji McIsaac/Getty Images
Page 107 © John Walder
Page 108 © Noah Graham
Pages 110–111 © Devin Allen
Page 112 © Khristopher "Squint" Sandifer
Page 115 © 2009 NBAE (Photo by Nathaniel S. Butler/NBAE via Getty Images)
Page 119 © Khristopher "Squint" Sandifer
Pages 120–121 © John Walder
Page 122 © 2010 NBAE (Photo by Rocky Widner/NBAE via Getty Images)
Pages 124–125 © Khristopher "Squint" Sandifer
Page 127 © Khristopher "Squint" Sandifer
Page 128 © Noah Graham
Page 130 © 2009 NBAE (Photo by Rocky Widner/NBAE via Getty Images)
Pages 132–133 © Khristopher "Squint" Sandifer
Page 134 © Photo by Sporting News via Getty Images
Page 135 © Noah Graham
Page 137 © Khristopher "Squint" Sandifer
Pages 138–139 © John Walder
Page 142 © Noah Graham
Page 145 © Photo by Gary Dineen/NBAE via Getty Images
Page 146a © Photo by Streeter Lecka/Getty Images
Page 146b © Photo by Kevin C. Cox/Getty Images
Page 146c © Photo by Gregory Shamus/Getty Images
Page 146d © Photo by Steve Dykes/Getty Images
Page 149 © Illustration by No Ideas with Nicolas Ardeley
Page 151 © John Walder
Pages 152–153 © Khristopher "Squint" Sandifer
Pages 154–155 © Khristopher "Squint" Sandifer
Page 156 (top) © Khristopher "Squint" Sandifer
Page 156 (bottom) © Devin Allen
Page 158 © Photo by Marlin Levison/Star Tribune via Getty Images
Page 159 © 2010 NBAE (Photo by David Sherman/NBAE via Getty Images)
Page 161 © Khristopher "Squint" Sandifer
Page 162 (top left) © 2016 NBAE (Photo by Garrett Ellwood/NBAE via Getty Images)
Page 162 (top right) © Photo by Ezra Shaw/Getty Images
Page 162 (center) © Photo by Ezra Shaw/Getty Images
Page 162 (bottom left) © 2016 NBAE (Photo by Noah Graham/NBAE via Getty Images)
Page 162 (bottom right) © Photo by Ezra Shaw/Getty Images
Page 163 (top left) © Photo by Thearon W. Henderson/Getty Images

Page 163 (top right) © 2015 NBAE (Photo by Noah Graham/NBAE via Getty Images)
Page 163 (bottom left) © 2015 NBAE (Photo by Noah Graham/NBAE via Getty Images)
Page 163 (bottom right) © Noah Graham
Page 165 © Khristopher "Squint" Sandifer
Page 166 © Khristopher "Squint" Sandifer
Page 168 © Khristopher "Squint" Sandifer
Pages 170–171 © Khristopher "Squint" Sandifer
Page 172 © Khristopher "Squint" Sandifer
Pages 176–177 © Photo by Scott Strazzante/San Francisco Chronicle via Getty Images
Page 179 (top) © Khristopher "Squint" Sandifer
Page 179 (bottom) © Khristopher "Squint" Sandifer
Pages 180–181 © Khristopher "Squint" Sandifer
Page 182 © Khristopher "Squint" Sandifer
Pages 184–185 © Devin Allen
Page 186 © Khristopher "Squint" Sandifer
Pages 190–191 © Khristopher "Squint" Sandifer
Page 192 © Khristopher "Squint" Sandifer
Page 195 © Devin Allen
Pages 196–197 © Illustration by No Ideas with Nicolas Ardeley
Page 198 © Devin Allen
Page 199 © John Walder
Pages 200 © Khristopher "Squint" Sandifer
Pages 204–205 © 2017 NBAE (Photo by Garrett Ellwood/NBAE via Getty Images)
Page 206 © Photo by Thearon W. Henderson/Getty Images
Page 207 © Photo by Lachlan Cunningham/Getty Images
Pages 208–209 © Khristopher "Squint" Sandifer
Page 210 © Noah Graham
Page 211 © Noah Graham
Page 213 © 2018 NBAE (Photo by Garrett Ellwood/NBAE via Getty Images)
Page 214 © 2013 NBAE (Photo by Nathaniel S. Butler/NBAE via Getty Images)
Pages 216–217 © Khristopher "Squint" Sandifer
Page 218 © You Know Who Shot It! - Jordan "JSquared" Jimenez
Pages 220–221 © You Know Who Shot It! - Jordan "JSquared" Jimenez
Page 222 © Khristopher "Squint" Sandifer
Page 224 © Noah Graham
Page 225 © Nhat V. Meyer/Bay Area News Group (Photo by MediaNews Group/Bay Area News via Getty Images)
Pages 226–227 © John Walder
Page 228 © United to Beat Malaria
Page 229 © United to Beat Malaria
Pages 230–231 © Khristopher "Squint" Sandifer
Page 232 © John Walder
Page 235 © Khristopher "Squint" Sandifer
Page 237 © Photo by Daniel Gluskoter/Icon Sportswire/Corbis/Icon Sportswire via Getty Images
Pages 238–239 © Khristopher "Squint" Sandifer
Page 240 © Noah Graham
Page 241 © Noah Graham
Page 243 © Noah Graham
Pages 244–245 © Khristopher "Squint"

Sandifer

Page 246 © You Know Who Shot It! - Jordan "JSquared" Jimenez

Page 247 © You Know Who Shot It! - Jordan "JSquared" Jimenez

Page 248 © Khristopher "Squint" Sandifer

Page 250 © Khristopher "Squint" Sandifer

Page 251 © Khristopher "Squint" Sandifer

Page 252 © Khristopher "Squint" Sandifer

Page 253 © Khristopher "Squint" Sandifer

Page 255 © Khristopher "Squint" Sandifer

Page 256 (top) © Khristopher "Squint" Sandifer

Page 256 (bottom) © Khristopher "Squint" Sandifer

Page 257 Copyright 2015 NBAE (Photo by Noah Graham/NBAE via Getty Images)

Page 259 © 2016 NBAE (Photo by Joe Murphy/NBAE via Getty Images)

Page 261 © 2016 NBAE (Photo by Joe Murphy/NBAE via Getty Images)

Page 263 © 2015 NBAE (Photo by Noah Graham/NBAE via Getty Images)

Page 264–265 © Illustration by No Ideas with Nicolas Ardeley

Page 267 © Khristopher "Squint" Sandifer

Page 268 © Noah Graham

Page 269 © Noah Graham

Pages 272–273 © Khristopher "Squint" Sandifer

Page 275 © Khristopher "Squint" Sandifer

Page 276 © Khristopher "Squint" Sandifer

Page 277 © Khristopher "Squint" Sandifer

Pages 278–279 © Khristopher "Squint" Sandifer

Pages 280–281 © Khristopher "Squint" Sandifer

Page 282 © Noah Graham

Page 284 © You Know Who Shot It! - Jordan "JSquared" Jimenez

Page 285 © You Know Who Shot It! - Jordan "JSquared" Jimenez

Page 286 © Khristopher "Squint" Sandifer

Page 287 © Adobe Stock

Pages 288–289 © Khristopher "Squint" Sandifer

Page 291 © Khristopher "Squint" Sandifer

Page 292 © Khristopher "Squint" Sandifer

Page 293 © Noah Graham

Pages 294–295 © Photo by Jamie Sabau/Getty Images

Page 298 © Khristopher "Squint" Sandifer

Page 301 © Khristopher "Squint" Sandifer

Page 302 (top) © Devin Allen

Page 302 (bottom) © Noah Graham

Pages 304–305 © Khristopher "Squint" Sandifer

Pages 306–307 © Noah Graham

Page 308 © Noah Graham

Page 311 © Noah Graham

Page 312 © Khristopher "Squint" Sandifer

Page 313 © Khristopher "Squint" Sandifer

Page 314 © Khristopher "Squint" Sandifer

Pages 318–319 © Khristopher "Squint" Sandifer

Pages 320–321 © Khristopher "Squint" Sandifer

Page 322 © Noah Graham

Page 323 © Noah Graham

Pages 324–325 © Devin Allen

Page 326 © Noah Graham

Page 327 © Noah Graham

Page 329 © Noah Graham

Page 332 (top) © Noah Graham

Page 332 (bottom) © Noah Graham

Page 334 © Khristopher "Squint" Sandifer
Page 335 © Khristopher "Squint" Sandifer
Page 336 (top) © Noah Graham
Page 336 (bottom) © Noah Graham
Page 338 © Andre D. Wagner
Page 341 (top) © Noah Graham
Page 341 (bottom) © Photo by Ezra Shaw/Getty Images
Pages 342–343 © Noah Graham
Page 345 © Khristopher "Squint" Sandifer
Page 346 (top) © Khristopher "Squint" Sandifer
Page 346 (bottom) © Khristopher "Squint" Sandifer
Page 347 (top) © Khristopher "Squint" Sandifer
Page 347 (bottom) © Khristopher "Squint" Sandifer
Pages 348–349 © Khristopher "Squint" Sandifer
Page 350 © Devin Allen
Page 353 © Khristopher "Squint" Sandifer
Pages 354–355 © Khristopher "Squint" Sandifer
Page 357 © Khristopher "Squint" Sandifer
Page 358 © Noah Graham
Page 359 © Illustration by No Ideas, Noah Graham + Getty Images
Pages 360–361 © Khristopher "Squint" Sandifer
Page 362 (top) © 2021 NBAE (Photo by Evan Yu/NBAE via Getty Images)
Page 362 (bottom) © Photo by Al Bello/Getty Images
Pages 366–367 © Khristopher "Squint" Sandifer
Page 369 © You Know Who Shot It! - Jordan "JSquared" Jimenez

Pages 370–371 © Khristopher "Squint" Sandifer
Page 372 © You Know Who Shot It! - Jordan "JSquared" Jimenez
Page 375 © You Know Who Shot It! - Jordan "JSquared" Jimenez
Pages 376–377 © Photo by Elsa/Getty Images
Page 379 © Noah Graham
Page 380 © Khristopher "Squint" Sandifer
Page 381 © 2023 NBAE (Photo by Jesse D. Garrabrant/NBAE via Getty Images)
Page 383 © Khristopher "Squint" Sandifer
Pages 384–385 © Khristopher "Squint" Sandifer
Page 386 © Khristopher "Squint" Sandifer
Page 387 © Khristopher "Squint" Sandifer
Page 389 © Khristopher "Squint" Sandifer
Page 390 (top) © Devin Allen
Page 390 (bottom) © Devin Allen
Page 395 © Adobe Stock
Page 396 © Khristopher "Squint" Sandifer
Page 399 © Khristopher "Squint" Sandifer
Page 400 © Khristopher "Squint" Sandifer
Pages 402–403 © Photo by Jamie Squire/Getty Images
Page 404 © Khristopher "Squint" Sandifer

Front and back endpapers
© Khristopher "Squint" Sandifer